The Lazy Investor's Playbook

The Lazy Investor's Playbook

The Art of Building Wealth by Doing Less Than You Think and More Than You Know

Elliot Wren

Mindful Pages

Published in 2025

ISBN: 9789371777001 (PB)
ISBN: 9789371779050 (eBook)

Published by

Mindful Pages
Imprint of Alpha Editions LLC
312 W. 2nd St #1834
Casper, WY 82601, USA

This book was developed using advanced writing tools to support the drafting and ideation process. All content has been thoughtfully curated, refined, and reviewed to ensure quality and relevance.

Content

Introduction
The Wisdom of Doing Less

There is a certain type of person for whom the notion of doing nothing is almost unbearable. Perhaps that resonates with you. You check the markets over coffee, tap your investing app while waiting for the lift, refresh news feeds in search of some edge. You convince yourself that this vigilance is necessary—that awareness equals intelligence, and intelligence is the path to wealth. Somewhere deep down, you hope that by paying closer attention, making just the right adjustment, you might finally stay ahead. And yet, despite all this motion, something persistent lingers: fatigue, confusion, and a nagging sense that you are no closer to either peace or prosperity than you were a year ago.

This book confronts that feeling directly. *The Lazy Investor's Playbook* is no compendium of shortcuts, hacks, or windfall strategies. It is something rarer: a reorientation of how we conceive wealth, effort, and control. At its core lies a provocative proposition: in investing, less is more—not as a quaint aphorism, but as a principle central to enduring success.

Modern investing culture is built on motion. Clicks, trades, alerts, streams of data, endless opinions—you are expected to act on them all. Passivity is portrayed as negligence; stillness, as incompetence. Yet what if that restlessness itself is the problem? What if the constant striving to optimise and outperform is not merely unhelpful, but actively harmful?

This book begins with a quiet, radical thesis: wealth favours the intentional mind, not the busiest hands. The most successful investors are rarely those who know the most or act the fastest. They are those who have learned to wait. They design systems requiring minimal supervision, distinguish discipline from interference, and recognise that emotional calm is not a byproduct of success—it is a prerequisite.

There are no hot stock tips here. You will not be taught candlestick patterns, market timing, or hedge fund strategies. Instead, you will be offered something far more durable: a framework to detach security from the noise of performance and align your money with your life—not the reverse.

To be clear, *The Lazy Investor's Playbook* is not for the indifferent. Laziness here is not inertia born of apathy. It is the discipline of selective effort, the wisdom to know what not to do, and the humility to allow time and structure to work for you. It is about building something so resilient that stepping back feels safe. Lazy, in this context, means free.

We inhabit an era that glorifies optimisation. Every aspect of life—from fitness to finance—is gamified, measured, and tracked. Productivity has become a moral virtue. Investors are caught in this loop, urged to refine, respond, and intervene. Yet frequent intervention carries a hidden cost. Empirical evidence repeatedly shows that overtrading erodes returns. The more we meddle, the more friction, error, and emotional sabotage we introduce. And yet the myth of the hyper-competent, ever-active investor persists—because we have been conditioned to equate effort with reward.

This conditioning is deeply historical. The Protestant work ethic, industrial ideals of diligence, and the mythos of self-made success all cultivate a worldview in which inactivity feels immoral. Yet markets are indifferent. They reward patience far more reliably than intervention. Simplicity scales; robustness trumps precision.

Across this book, you will encounter a counterintuitive but liberating perspective: an elegantly designed, automated, emotionally detached investment system is not only effective—it aligns with a life of clarity, purpose, and peace. Strategic stillness—what we term "doing nothing with intention"—often outperforms anxious hustle.

We begin by dismantling the illusion of control that drives frantic investment behaviour. Chapter One explores the psychological compulsion to intervene, revealing how fear and uncertainty generate actions that feel rational but rarely are. Subsequent chapters examine the power of inertia, the emotional dividend curve, and portfolio design that thrives in your absence.

Later sections address time as the ultimate asset, the hidden psychological rewards of automation, and the emotional tax imposed by overinformation. We challenge conventional definitions of performance, offering instead a vision of wealth framed by sufficiency rather than supremacy.

This is not abstract theory. It is grounded in behavioural economics, empirical data, and the lived experience of long-term investors. Beyond the evidence lies a more enduring lesson: true wealth is not a number or benchmark. It is a relationship—with time, with sufficiency, and with your own nervous system.

To invest well is not to outthink the market. It is to outgrow the illusion that you must.

There is something undeniably seductive about constant involvement: monitoring markets, making trades, forecasting. It feels powerful. Yet much of this is theatre. Real work occurs in design, not daily decision-making. Once a system is sound, the most valuable trait is restraint—rarely celebrated, often overlooked.

Stillness, in finance, is a superpower. Misunderstood and maligned, inaction is often mistaken for ignorance. Yet the greatest control lies in knowing when to relinquish it. This book invites a form of confidence not born of bravado but of assurance—a calm rooted in design, not prediction, structure, not hustle.

The chapters ahead will teach you to construct that system—mentally, emotionally, practically. You will learn to filter noise, reframe risk, and define success on your terms. More profoundly, you will be asked: what kind of life are you optimising for?

Ultimately, money is not the goal. Freedom is. And freedom, as you will discover, begins with the courage to do less.

Welcome to *The Lazy Investor's Playbook*. Let's begin.

Chapter 1
The Illusion of Control

There is a peculiar comfort in believing we are in control. To think that every action we take directly shapes our outcomes, that effort naturally produces security, is deeply reassuring. It flatters the ego, eases our fear of randomness, and in many areas of life—career, study, even physical training—this worldview holds some truth: work harder, practice longer, and improvement usually follows. Investing, however, is different. Here, effort rarely guarantees results; often, trying harder is counterproductive.

This chapter opens with an uncomfortable observation: behaviours that feel industrious in finance often undermine performance. Markets reward structure, not energy. They respond to humility, not hustle. And yet the archetype of the hyper-alert investor persists—someone who reads financial news at dawn, monitors positions relentlessly, reacts instantly to trends. Media and popular culture celebrate this image: the sharp, decisive trader who bends the market through sheer intelligence and tenacity.

Its persistence is understandable. The fantasy that attention and precision can bend markets to our will is emotionally seductive. We crave control in an inherently uncertain world. Yet the data tell a different story—volatility, underperformance, and stress are far more common than triumph.

Why do we cling to this myth? Partly psychology. Humans are wired for agency. In uncertainty, inaction feels dangerous. Market dips trigger primal alarms in our nervous systems; losses feel like threats, not numbers. Passivity becomes guilt-inducing. Modern culture amplifies this: frequent trading signals engagement and competence; restraint signals disengagement or ignorance. Action is rewarded for appearance, not outcome.

Empirical evidence is clear. Numerous studies show that frequent trading correlates with lower returns. Barber and Odean, analysing thousands of retail investors, found that the most active traders consistently earned less than the least active. Hyperactivity, driven by confidence and real-time data, does not yield advantage; it creates interference. Even professional fund managers often fail to outperform low-cost, passive benchmarks over time. Markets are complex adaptive systems—less like clockwork, more like weather. Noise confounds signal, and meddling increases friction, fees, and timing errors, repeatedly interrupting compounding's quiet power.

At the heart of this is a misunderstanding of control. True financial control comes from intentional restraint, not constant engagement. Think of it like gardening versus fiddling. A gardener plants, tends patiently, and trusts the process. A fiddler tugs at roots daily and wonders why nothing grows. In finance, wealth is cultivated, not chased.

Much of what passes for strategy is coping: selling after a dip is often fear, buying a rally is herd psychology. Investing becomes a theatre of anxieties, revealing our relationship with uncertainty, identity, and control. The market itself is unpredictable short-term, reflexive mid-term, and generous long-term—but only to those who endure. Staying power demands resisting the urge to act when every instinct screams otherwise. This is the art of doing nothing.

Doing nothing is not apathy; it is strategic stillness. It is building systems robust enough to endure turbulence without constant interference, trusting them even amid temporary underperformance, and decoupling emotion from market swings. It is a radical inversion of conventional advice: step back rather than tune in, design for volatility rather than chase it, become indifferent to beating the market because process matters more than outcomes.

Strategic stillness requires intentional inaction—knowing when intervention adds value, and when it soothes anxiety. It demands self-awareness, patience, and humility: humility to accept that markets ignore effort, that intelligence without discipline is dangerous, that much of what we call strategy is noise.

In this chapter, we examine the myth of the active investor, studying those who failed through excess and those who succeeded through deliberate restraint. We review psychological research on action bias, control illusions, and the perils of overconfidence. We explore how fear drives premature decisions and how emotional regulation, more than prediction, shapes long-term results.

Ultimately, the most successful investors are defined not by what they do, but by what they refrain from doing. They know how to wait, when to abstain, and how to structure portfolios to respect reality. If the world labels this laziness, so be it. You will recognise it as mastery. In a domain addicted to more, doing less is not just contrarian—it is correct. The illusion of control is seductive, but relinquishing it offers freedom. This chapter invites a new clarity, one that begins in the stillness between decisions.

The Myth of the Active Hero

The cult of the active investor is one of the most enduring and seductive illusions in modern finance. This figure—the tireless analyst, the ever-tuned-in strategist, the sharp-suited protagonist who outpaces the market with intelligence and agility—is not just a fixture of popular culture. He is the personification of a deeper cultural bias: the belief that more action equals more control, and that control guarantees success. We celebrate him in films, in finance columns, and in the collective mythology of modern capitalism. But strip away the narrative gloss, and a stark truth emerges: the active hero is far more fiction than fact.

Despite the reverence surrounding the hyperactive investor archetype, empirical evidence has mounted for decades against its core assumptions. The data does not merely suggest that active trading underperforms; it shows it consistently, across timeframes, geographies, and investor types. Study after study—whether conducted in academia or within the walls of major financial institutions—confirms the same uncomfortable pattern: the more one trades, the worse one tends to do. And yet, the illusion persists.

This persistence cannot be explained by ignorance alone. The average investor today has more access to financial research, portfolio tools, and data than any previous generation. Passive index investing—boring, patient, unglamorous—has become not only popular but mainstream. Still, the gravitational pull of action remains strong. Investors tweak allocations after watching a market segment rally. They sell on fear and buy on euphoria. They convince themselves that vigilance is a virtue, and that sitting still is somehow irresponsible.

To understand why this myth holds such power, we must look beyond logic. The active investor is not merely a strategic figure; he is a psychological one. He offers a fantasy—of mastery over chaos, of skill triumphing over randomness, of self-determination in a system that otherwise feels opaque and unresponsive. This fantasy is not just compelling; it is soothing. It shields us from the discomfort of admitting how little control we truly have in the face of global economic complexity.

At the heart of this behaviour is a deeply human instinct: the need to act under uncertainty. When markets fall, inaction feels like neglect. When headlines scream volatility, passivity feels like cowardice. Doing something—*anything*—is emotionally validating, even if it's financially irrational. This is known in behavioural finance as "action bias," a cognitive distortion that causes individuals to favour doing over waiting, even when evidence favours restraint. It is a bias that evolution has likely baked into us; after all, in the ancestral environment, failing to act under threat could mean death. But in the financial markets, acting out of reflex often equates to self-sabotage.

Consider the findings of a well-known study by Brad Barber and Terrance Odean, who examined over 60,000 retail trading accounts over a six-year period. Their conclusion was unambiguous: the investors who traded the most earned the least. The top quintile of active traders underperformed the market by a wide margin, even before accounting for transaction costs. After costs, the gap widened into a chasm. Interestingly, the researchers also noted that these hyperactive traders displayed high levels of overconfidence—

another hallmark of the active hero myth. They believed they were outperforming, when in fact, they were doing measurable harm to their portfolios.

The narrative of the market-beating maverick is reinforced not just by films and finance media, but by a broader societal ideology that equates visibility with competence. We assume that the investor who is constantly adjusting positions, explaining strategies, and publishing predictions must know something we do not. They appear confident, articulate, and informed. Their complexity feels like sophistication. But sophistication, in markets, is often just noise dressed in expensive language. Simplicity, not intricacy, is what tends to endure.

This is not to suggest that all active management is futile. There are, of course, investors who outperform over long time horizons. But they are the statistical outliers, not the norm. Even among professionals—mutual fund managers, hedge fund operators, and institutional asset managers—the majority fail to beat passive benchmarks after fees. The SPIVA (S&P Indices Versus Active) scorecards, published annually, are especially damning. Over a 15-year horizon, more than 85% of actively managed large-cap funds underperform their index counterparts. And this underperformance is not simply cyclical; it is structural.

Why, then, does the myth endure? Because it offers an identity. The active investor is not merely doing finance; he is *being* someone decisive, engaged, elite. The allure lies not just in the outcome, but in the self-image. It is emotionally more gratifying to *try* and fail than to do nothing and feel inert. The markets, in this frame, become a proving ground—not just of strategy, but of self-worth.

There is also the matter of attention. In a media ecosystem saturated with noise, passive investing does not lend itself to headlines. "Investor holds same allocation for 10 years" is not a story that sells. But "Tech stock surge triggers smart money shift" captures eyeballs, generates ad revenue, and fuels the machine. In this environment, doing less is not only countercultural—it is invisible.

The consequences of buying into this myth are not limited to underperformance. They include increased stress, reduced life satisfaction, and a distorted relationship with money. Investors who internalise the need to constantly outperform often live in a state of permanent vigilance—checking markets daily, reacting to news cycles, chasing the next edge. This state of mind is exhausting, and rarely rewarded.

Yet perhaps the most insidious aspect of the active hero myth is that it creates a false dichotomy between engagement and success. The truth is more nuanced. The most effective investors are not disengaged—they are highly engaged *in design*, but disengaged *in execution*. They front-load their thinking, create robust systems, automate intelligently, and then step back. Their skill lies not in their reaction speed, but in their willingness to trust the plan.

To embrace this mindset is to adopt what this book calls strategic stillness. It is not passive in the pejorative sense; it is selective in its action. It involves clarity of purpose, discipline in allocation, and serenity in the face of short-term volatility. It is rooted in the understanding that markets are not puzzles to be solved daily, but ecosystems to be navigated over decades.

The myth of the active hero flatters our ego and justifies our fears. It offers the illusion that we can outperform risk by anticipating it, that we can earn certainty through effort. But the market is not a problem to be outworked. It is a system to be understood, respected, and—above all—left alone when the temptation to meddle is strongest.

Let go of the fantasy. The real heroes in investing are not those who move fast, but those who wait well. Not those who chase edges, but those who build margins. Not those who need to be seen, but those who are content to be right *eventually*.

In this reframing lies your advantage. Not by becoming louder, quicker, or more informed—but by becoming quieter, slower, and more deliberate than the market expects. By rejecting the myth of the active hero, you begin to unlearn the noise—and in doing so, start hearing the signal.

Busy Doesn't Mean Better

The financial world, like much of modern life, rewards visibility and motion. To be seen constantly managing, analysing, and adjusting is often mistaken for competence. In investing, this illusion of productivity takes a particular shape: the busy investor. Eyes always on the screen, mind forever on the next move, he views every lull in market activity as a call to action. But beneath the confident gestures lies a contradiction too large to ignore: the busier an investor becomes, the more their returns tend to suffer.

This is not a philosophical position; it is a documented statistical reality. Across decades of empirical research, one finding recurs with unsettling consistency—frequent trading erodes performance. The data are neither subtle nor marginal. They are wide-ranging and decisive, undermining the common belief that staying active in the markets correlates with superior outcomes. In fact, the opposite tends to be true. Activity is often inversely correlated with returns, and the reasons are not technical—they are psychological.

Consider the evidence from one of the most widely cited studies in behavioural finance, conducted by Brad Barber and Terrance Odean. Analysing over 66,000 retail brokerage accounts from 1991 to 1996, they found that the most active traders significantly underperformed those who traded the least. Before accounting for transaction costs, high-frequency traders already earned lower gross returns; after costs, their underperformance became stark. The least active traders earned an annual net return of 18.5%, while the most active group earned just 11.4%. This wasn't a temporary blip or a one-off anomaly—it was systemic.

Importantly, this wasn't a study of uneducated speculators. These were everyday investors, many of whom believed they were applying sound judgement. But they shared a critical flaw: the belief that constant vigilance would lead to better outcomes. This belief, as it turns out, is driven more by emotion than logic.

The psychological need to intervene—to make a change, to assert control—is one of the most powerful forces in investor behaviour. It emerges from the discomfort of uncertainty. When portfolio values fluctuate, the instinctive reaction is to respond. Humans are not wired to sit still in the face of perceived threat; evolution favoured those who acted under duress. In markets, however, this trait becomes maladaptive. Volatility is not necessarily a signal of danger, but the brain interprets it as such. As a result, investors intervene prematurely, selling during downturns and buying during rallies—exactly the opposite of what logic prescribes.

Action, in this context, becomes a form of self-soothing. The investor doesn't necessarily trade because conditions demand it, but because *doing something* feels better than doing nothing. This is the emotional equivalent of fiddling with a thermostat every five minutes to feel in control, even if it makes the temperature less stable. Financial decision-making, when untethered from discipline, begins to resemble anxiety management rather than strategy.

What complicates matters further is that the market occasionally rewards this behaviour, at least in the short term. A well-timed trade, a lucky exit, a sudden windfall—these intermittent rewards reinforce the illusion that intervention works. Behavioural scientists refer to this as "variable reinforcement," the same mechanism that keeps gamblers pulling the lever. It creates a psychological hook, one that is immune to contradictory evidence. The mind doesn't weigh the long-term average; it fixates on the occasional win. This selective memory reinforces the illusion of skill where there is mostly noise.

The brokerage industry, for its part, has historically done little to discourage this behaviour. Revenue models often benefit from trading volume. Until recently, commissions were the lifeblood of retail brokerages, incentivising platforms to encourage more transactions, not fewer. Even with the shift to commission-free models, the attention economy continues to thrive on engagement. Trading apps now emulate social media—flashing alerts, offering "trending" tickers, gamifying portfolios with animations and dopamine-driven interfaces. These are not tools for building wealth; they are psychological traps designed to stimulate action.

Yet it is not only retail investors who fall prey to this mindset. Many professional fund managers engage in high-frequency rebalancing, sector shifts, and tactical rotations under the banner of "active management." But study after study shows that, over long horizons, most fail to outperform their benchmarks. According to S&P's SPIVA scorecard, over 80% of actively managed large-cap funds underperform the S&P 500 over a 15-year period. The few who outperform often struggle to repeat their success, raising difficult questions about how much of that performance was attributable to skill versus randomness.

One might argue that being busy at least protects against major losses—that vigilance can prevent catastrophe. But the historical record suggests otherwise. During periods of crisis, such as the 2008 financial collapse or the COVID-19 market plunge in early 2020, the investors who fared best were often those who *didn't* react. Those who maintained consistent contributions, rebalanced infrequently, and refrained from panic-selling typically emerged with stronger long-term performance. Resisting the urge to flee during drawdowns is not passive neglect—it is a deliberate, often difficult act of emotional maturity.

The uncomfortable truth is that long-term investing success is rarely a function of frequent decision-making. It is the outcome of setting intelligent policies and sticking to them—through noise, headlines, and fear. Strategic asset allocation, disciplined rebalancing, and consistent saving do far more for wealth accumulation than any collection of reactive trades. The skill lies in construction, not in constant recalibration.

But to adopt this mindset requires a redefinition of what it means to be "engaged" as an investor. Engagement is not measured by the number of trades executed or hours spent analysing charts. It is better understood as the care invested in building a thoughtful, resilient system—one that needs minimal intervention because it was designed to withstand both volatility and inattention. A low-touch portfolio is not a product of laziness; it is the culmination of intelligent design.

This reframing is not only practical but liberating. It frees the investor from the exhausting burden of staying perpetually informed, tuned-in, and responsive. It allows time and attention to be redirected toward life itself—toward career, family, health, creativity. It acknowledges that the highest form of financial control may in fact lie in knowing when *not* to interfere.

And yet, the temptation to act will always remain. It is psychological, social, and increasingly technological. Investors today are bombarded by real-time data, algorithmic nudges, and a 24/7 news cycle engineered for adrenaline. In this environment, resisting the impulse to intervene is not a matter of willpower alone. It is a practice—one that must be supported by structure, rules, and self-awareness.

The most effective antidote is to shift focus from performance to process. When attention is rooted in a system rather than an outcome, the need to react diminishes. This is the essence of strategic stillness. It is not about avoiding action altogether, but about ensuring that action is rare, intentional, and rule-based.

What distinguishes the successful investor from the merely busy one is not intelligence, access, or even temperament—it is clarity. Clarity about what matters, what moves the needle, and what can safely be ignored. It is the ability to separate true risk from temporary noise, and to build an approach that honours this distinction.

Being busy in the markets may feel noble. It may look intelligent. But the results are often quietly devastating. The question worth asking is not "Am I doing enough?" but rather "Am I doing too much?" Because in the world of investing, *enough* is a far more powerful concept than *more*.

The investor who learns to be deliberate, who resists the pull of activity for its own sake, does more than improve performance. They reclaim their time, their attention, and their peace of mind. And in the end, these may be the most valuable returns of all.

Control as a Coping Mechanism

There is no greater discomfort in finance than the feeling of helplessness. The idea that your savings—years of work, discipline, and sacrifice—can be impacted by factors entirely outside your control is not merely inconvenient. It is existential. It creates the same kind of unease that drives people to religious fundamentalism, conspiracy theories, or compulsive routines: the desperate need to believe that uncertainty can be tamed. In the world of investing, this need expresses itself through the illusion of control—through charts, predictions, strategies, and endless decisions masquerading as mastery. But look more closely, and it becomes clear: many of these actions are not truly strategic. They are psychological coping mechanisms.

The financial markets are among the most complex systems humans have ever created—interconnected, adaptive, and constantly shifting. Prices respond to news, sentiment, algorithms, global politics, weather, war, and panic. Despite this, most investors—amateur and professional alike—harbour a deep-seated belief that if they pay enough attention, run the right models, or act quickly enough, they can pre-empt the chaos. But the market does not reward certainty. It rewards resilience. And this distinction is more than semantic. It speaks to the very heart of why we act the way we do with money.

Behavioural finance has long observed that what feels rational is often emotionally motivated. This is especially evident during periods of market stress. When markets fall, few investors calmly reassess their long-term allocations. Instead, they grasp for action—selling assets, switching funds, hoarding cash—because these behaviours *feel* like protection. The discomfort of uncertainty drives a scramble for certainty, even if that certainty is fictional. The irony is brutal: the more we act to soothe our anxiety, the more we compromise our outcomes.

This phenomenon is not confined to financial novices. During the 2008 global financial crisis, institutional portfolios saw massive drawdowns not because managers lacked skill, but because they capitulated to fear. In one study, researchers found that many pension and endowment funds reallocated heavily to bonds and cash near market bottoms, only to miss the sharp recovery that followed. Their decisions were not grounded in macroeconomic insight. They were driven by boardroom panic, media saturation, and a fundamental discomfort with unpredictability.

What these examples illustrate is a profound behavioural reality: *many financial decisions are made not to improve performance, but to reduce emotional discomfort.* The action may be presented as logical, but its true function is psychological. This is why investors often break their own rules in moments of crisis. It's not a failure of intelligence. It's a failure of emotional architecture.

Control, in this sense, becomes a proxy for safety. To sell a falling asset, to rotate into a "safe haven," or to rebalance in response to headlines is not always about returns—it is about narrative. If we can tell ourselves a story about why we're acting, we can reclaim a sense of agency. The danger lies in mistaking that story for strategy.

Part of this compulsion is rooted in our evolutionary psychology. The human brain is wired for pattern recognition and survival. In ancient environments, uncertain conditions meant threat—storms, predators, famine. Action in the face of uncertainty was adaptive. But in markets, where randomness and noise are pervasive, the same instinct leads us astray. We see trends where none exist. We act to prevent losses that may never materialise. And we believe, with quiet desperation, that our intervention will protect us.

This coping impulse is further reinforced by the architecture of modern finance. The tools available to the everyday investor—apps, dashboards, newsfeeds—create an illusion of agency. Real-time data streams, performance graphs, and alerts suggest that the market is a controllable interface rather than a probabilistic system. The more information we see, the more we believe we understand. The more we believe we understand, the more compelled we feel to act. It is a dangerous feedback loop.

Yet, paradoxically, the most successful investors are those who design systems precisely so they *don't* have to intervene. They understand that discomfort is not a signal—it's background noise. They build portfolios that can absorb shocks, rather than react to them. And they adopt a different mental posture: one that accepts uncertainty as normal, not exceptional. This is not apathy; it is sophistication. It is the recognition that the desire for certainty is natural, but the pursuit of it through constant intervention is futile.

There is a moral dimension to this as well. In our desire to exert control, we risk becoming short-sighted. We prioritise short-term certainty over long-term growth. We seek relief over resilience. This is the psychological equivalent of selling one's future for emotional convenience. But investing is not therapy. The market does not care about our comfort. It rewards patience, not panic; structure, not spontaneity.

The discomfort investors feel is real, and it should not be dismissed. But it must be redirected. Rather than acting to suppress that discomfort, it must be acknowledged, studied, and anticipated. This is where true investment wisdom begins: with emotional literacy. The ability to observe one's fear without obeying it. The clarity to distinguish noise from necessity. And the discipline to stay the course, even when the impulse to deviate feels overwhelming.

This is why strategic stillness, introduced earlier in this chapter, is not merely a behavioural recommendation—it is a psychological stance. It reframes the act of doing nothing as an assertion of control, not a surrender of it. It says: *I have already built a structure that anticipates uncertainty. I do not need to respond to every shadow that passes across the wall.*

When control is no longer used as a balm for anxiety, it can be repurposed into something more valuable: design. The investor's real control lies not in their ability to react, but in their ability to architect systems that render reactions unnecessary. This requires a shift in identity—from market participant to system steward. From anxious responder to thoughtful constructor.

The market is, by definition, a place of uncertainty. That is its nature, not its flaw. Every moment spent trying to eliminate that uncertainty is a moment diverted from what truly matters—defining clear goals, setting intelligent parameters, and trusting the process. The investor who internalises this does not chase forecasts or flinch at volatility. They know that their need for control is not a financial requirement but an emotional habit. And like all habits, it can be transformed.

To mature as an investor is to stop mistaking control for wisdom. It is to see that most financial errors are not rooted in ignorance, but in emotional displacement. The investor acts not because they must—but because they cannot sit with their fear.

Reclaiming that stillness—conscious, constructed, and unshaken—is not only the antidote to overreaction. It is the foundation of durable wealth. Not because it guarantees better outcomes, but because it prevents the kinds of self-inflicted wounds that ruin otherwise sound strategies. The market will always be uncertain. That part cannot be changed. But how we relate to that uncertainty—whether we fight it, fear it, or design around it—is entirely within our control.

When Doing Nothing Is a Skill

The modern investor is bombarded with messages that imply urgency is synonymous with intelligence. Every push notification, market update, and talking head implies that something must be done. Now. The idea that one could simply hold a position, ignore the noise, and walk away feels counterintuitive, even reckless. And yet, the most enduring truth in investing is also the one least emotionally satisfying: *doing nothing is often the most intelligent action an investor can take.*

Stillness, in the financial context, is frequently mistaken for negligence. It carries connotations of laziness, indifference, or ignorance. But this interpretation reflects a profound misunderstanding of both markets and human behaviour. The truth is that sustained inaction, when chosen consciously and anchored in structure, is one of the most advanced forms of investment discipline. It requires not only foresight and conviction, but a deep understanding of how markets function and how minds react under pressure.

This is the foundation of what we call *strategic stillness*—a deliberate, rule-based decision to abstain from unnecessary action, not because one is passive, but because one has already acted with clarity. It is a skill that involves resisting the compulsion to react, not out of laziness, but because the reaction itself would degrade performance, introduce friction, or distort a well-designed plan. Strategic stillness is not the absence of involvement. It is the presence of trust—in the system, in the process, and in the long arc of rational design.

To appreciate the depth of this idea, we must first untangle the powerful cultural biases that shape our relationship with action.

Western societies, particularly those shaped by industrial and post-industrial capitalism, place extraordinary value on productivity. Time is money. Efficiency is virtue. Movement is equated with improvement. These assumptions have been internalised so completely that even silence or pause is often filled with background noise—a podcast, a screen, a scan of headlines. In this environment, inaction feels like abdication. But this is a psychological mirage.

In financial markets, action is not always additive. In fact, it is often destructive. Trading introduces costs: transaction fees, bid-ask spreads, taxes, and the more subtle but powerful cost of timing errors. More critically, it opens the door to behavioural pitfalls: loss aversion, anchoring, confirmation bias, and overconfidence. By acting frequently, the investor does not optimise outcomes; they compound error. The empirical data confirms this with brutal consistency.

Consider the research conducted by Fidelity's behavioural analytics team, which once undertook an internal study to determine which accounts had performed best over a multi-year horizon. The surprising finding? Many of the top-performing accounts belonged to investors who had *forgotten they had accounts at all.* The absence of activity—forced by forgetfulness—had shielded them from emotional responses and impulsive decisions. They had, in effect, stumbled upon strategic stillness.

What makes inaction difficult is not ignorance, but intelligence misapplied. The smarter the investor, the more prone they are to overfitting narratives, reading into data, and second-guessing plans. Markets encourage the illusion that there's always a right move waiting to be uncovered—some hidden signal amidst the noise. But what looks like insight is often randomness. Acting on it can erode the very advantage that long-term investors possess: time in the market.

This becomes especially clear during periods of high volatility. When markets fall sharply, the instinct to "take control" by selling is overwhelming. When they rise rapidly, the fear of missing out fuels reactive buying. In both scenarios, action feels rational. But history shows us the contrary. Investors who stayed fully invested during drawdowns consistently outperformed those who tried to time exits and re-entries. Missing just a handful of the market's best-performing days can permanently damage long-term returns—and those days often occur immediately after the worst ones.

The investor who develops the skill of stillness understands this not as a theoretical point, but as a functional truth. They design their portfolios not to avoid volatility, but to absorb it. They align their expectations with long-term horizons, not short-term gratification. And most importantly, they cultivate the inner discipline to remain unmoved by movements that demand attention but not action.

Strategic stillness also requires the suppression of ego. In a world that equates success with mastery, the idea that "doing less" might be superior grates against the identity of the high-achiever. This is why inaction is often psychologically harder for professionals and experts than for novices. The more one knows, the more one feels obligated to *do* something with that knowledge. But markets are not machines to be operated; they are systems to be navigated. The illusion of control is often stronger in those who believe they understand it best.

What, then, does strategic stillness actually look like in practice? It begins with structure: clear asset allocation, regular but infrequent rebalancing, automated contributions, and predefined rules about when and how to adjust. It includes removing triggers for unnecessary action—unsubscribing from market news alerts, limiting account checks, and replacing reactive habits with reflective ones. And it is reinforced by accountability: written plans, peer review, or professional guidance that reduces the emotional burden of standing still when every signal says move.

This form of stillness is not intuitive, but it is trainable. Like any discipline, it improves with practice and repetition. Investors can rehearse it through simulated scenarios, post-mortem analyses, and the cultivation of what psychologist Walter Mischel called "cool cognition"—a state of deliberate, emotionally detached thinking under stress. Over time, the discomfort of inaction fades, replaced by something rarer and more valuable: calm confidence in the face of noise.

The benefits of strategic stillness extend beyond the portfolio. They include reduced stress, more time for meaningful pursuits, and a healthier relationship with money. When one is no longer emotionally tethered to the tick-by-tick fluctuations of markets, space opens up—for creativity, relationships, reflection. Wealth becomes not a source of pressure, but a platform for stability.

Crucially, strategic stillness is not about avoiding decisions, but about relocating them. Instead of deciding *what to do now*, the skilled investor has already decided *what to do when*. That decision, made in a state of clarity, is infinitely more valuable than one made in reaction to stress. This is what distinguishes lazy investing as a high-discipline endeavour. It appears effortless on the surface, but only because the effort has already occurred—upstream, in design.

To invest well over decades requires a radical shift in mindset. Not from ignorance to knowledge, but from action to intention. The world will continue to reward those who appear busy. Markets will continue to punish those who mistake motion for mastery. But beneath this turbulence lies a deeper current—one available only to those who trust the silence of good design.

Doing nothing is not a failure of effort. It is evidence of foresight. It is a vote of confidence in your process, your principles, and your patience. And in a system built on noise, that kind of quiet is not just rare. It's a competitive advantage.

Chapter 2
In Praise of Inertia

When Sir Isaac Newton described inertia as a body's resistance to change unless acted upon by an external force, he spoke of physical objects. Yet the principle resonates with surprising elegance in finance. Capital, like a rolling stone, gains from continuity; every interruption diminishes momentum. In investing, inertia is not stagnation—it is stability. It is the quiet discipline of allowing a well-constructed system to operate uninterrupted, compounding steadily, while the anxious hand of its architect remains still.

This chapter opens with a provocative assertion: the optimal condition for a thoughtfully designed portfolio is motionless. Not passive, not indifferent, but mechanically aligned to a trajectory set with intelligence, moving forward under the unseen power of compounding. What outsiders perceive as disengagement is, in reality, deliberate restraint—an art that preserves energy and shields the investor from unnecessary drag.

Energy, after all, is finite. Inertia conserves it. Every adjustment, however minor, imposes a hidden cost: financial friction, emotional churn, missteps, and fees accumulate silently, eroding the benefits of compounding. The most damaging interventions are rarely the dramatic ones; they are small, frequent, seemingly rational changes that, over decades, sap performance.

Investors rarely intend self-sabotage. They tweak. A reallocation here, a slight shift there, a timing adjustment to earnings reports. Each move has logic, perhaps even a spreadsheet to justify it. Yet together, these minor interventions compound into friction. Conversely, those who generate wealth most consistently are not the most active or analytically precise—they are the ones who recognise how fragile exponential progress can be in the face of incessant meddling.

A pervasive fallacy in investing is the belief that performance correlates with proximity to information. "If I monitor more, I'll see patterns; if I act faster, I'll capture opportunity." Empirical evidence suggests otherwise. Over-engagement breeds reaction, not foresight. Investors who observe less often tend to make better long-term decisions, spared from the emotional cost of mistaking noise for signal.

Here, the physics metaphor proves illuminating. A system set on a sound trajectory requires energy merely to maintain momentum, not to be constantly redirected. Each change of course extracts a toll—momentum dissipates, turbulence arises, forward motion slows. Friction is invisible day-to-day, yet over decades it differentiates lasting wealth from middling outcomes.

Consider the disciplined investor who, in the early 2000s, built a globally diversified, low-cost portfolio with sensible equity-bond allocations, automatic contributions, and annual rebalancing. They do not react to crashes, chase trends, or overweight sectors based on headlines. Twenty years later, their returns surpass peers who made dozens of "rational" adjustments inspired by news, geopolitics, or tactical insight. The edge? Inertia.

This is not to deny change. Markets shift, circumstances evolve. But well-designed systems absorb volatility; they anticipate turbulence and reduce downstream decision-making. Diversification, liquidity buffers, and horizon-aware allocations create portfolios that breathe independently. The goal is not avoidance but upstream design: fewer reactive decisions, more structural integrity.

When faced with temptation to act, ask: am I addressing a genuine flaw, or reacting to discomfort? Strategy or psychology? These questions distinguish the tinkerer from the designer. Life rewards intervention; investing punishes it. The highest virtue in finance is restraint—the ability to let systems work without interference.

Emotionally, inaction is hard to defend. When markets surge, stillness feels like stagnation; when they fall, it feels negligent. A long-term lens—the decade filter—alters perspective. Decisions are assessed against ten-year horizons rather than daily fluctuations. Short-term noise fades, urgency diminishes, and calmer, more rational decision-making emerges. The decade filter is not abstract; it is a cognitive tool prioritising durability over brilliance, consistency over monthly wins.

Successful investors often appear mundane externally, yet their discipline is profound. Their rigor is embedded in design, not action. Portfolios are engineered to thrive independently, a testament to architectural intelligence. This is not romanticised passivity but informed, structural prudence: the cost of friction is high; the reward of stillness, compounding.

Inertia is not stagnation. It is letting good ideas run unmolested. It acknowledges that time, not talent, is the ultimate lever of wealth creation. It recognises that the most critical skill is avoiding the compulsion to outsmart oneself.

This chapter is an invitation: move from active management to architectural thinking. Build once, build well, and step aside. Trust the systems you've crafted and the silent mechanics of compounding. Here, in deliberate inaction, lies the mastery that most investors never attain—where doing nothing becomes the most skillful act of all.

The Physics of Money and Motion

If you were to study the long-term growth of a well-diversified investment portfolio and compare it to a physical object in motion, you would find an elegant overlap. In physics, inertia is defined as the resistance of a body to changes in its state of motion unless acted upon by an external force. The object stays its course—not because it is trying, but because that's how systems behave when left undisturbed. The same applies, almost uncannily, to compounding capital. Once a sound portfolio is set in motion, its greatest ally is uninterrupted trajectory. Intervene too often, and the system stutters. Allow it to run, and it compounds with quiet, powerful consistency.

The metaphor is not incidental. Inertia, in finance, is not about passivity. It is about momentum preserved. Just as a satellite in orbit requires no propulsion once properly launched, an intelligently designed portfolio needs little ongoing interference. What it does require is time—exposure to the full arc of market cycles without being diverted by human impatience or the illusion of improvement. It thrives on continuity, not reactivity. Yet most investors treat portfolios like vehicles that must be constantly steered, corrected, and accelerated. The unintended consequence is friction—hidden costs, lost returns, and psychological drag that accumulates over decades.

Friction in finance wears many guises. It is not just the obvious costs of brokerage fees, spreads, and taxes. It's also the opportunity cost of reallocation at the wrong time, the loss of compounding due to interrupted holding periods, and the erosion of conviction caused by too much exposure to irrelevant information. Each small "adjustment," made with the best of intentions, imposes a tiny cost. One or two may seem inconsequential. But over a thirty-year horizon, these micro-costs compound in the opposite direction of wealth—silently, steadily, and irreversibly.

Consider the case of long-term fund data from Vanguard and Morningstar. The investors who achieved the highest returns over two decades were not those who traded actively or responded nimbly to market changes. They were those who left their allocations largely untouched. Some rebalanced on an annual or biannual basis. Many made no changes at all. Their success was not due to market timing or tactical allocation—it was due to *staying the course.* Just as Newton's law describes, their financial trajectory remained intact because they allowed no external force—fear, hype, ego, or boredom—to alter its motion.

The trouble is that the human mind is not naturally wired to appreciate inertial systems. We are drawn to input-output relationships: if I act, I expect a result. If I intervene, I expect improvement. This is especially true in domains like work, sport, or study, where sustained effort usually correlates with enhanced performance. In those contexts, doing more is doing better. But financial markets invert this logic. There, *inaction is often more intelligent than action.* This inversion is deeply counterintuitive—and emotionally uncomfortable. It's why many investors struggle to leave their portfolios alone. It *feels* wrong.

The physics metaphor also highlights the importance of initial conditions. In mechanics, if you launch a projectile at the wrong angle, it will never reach its intended target—regardless of how long it flies. The same is true for investment portfolios. The upfront design—asset mix, time horizon, risk tolerance, and contribution strategy—is what determines whether inertia will serve or sabotage you. Inertia amplifies both good and bad decisions. If the structure is flawed, doing nothing will not save you. It will simply compound the flaw. But if the structure is sound, intervening can only get in the way.

This raises an essential distinction: *inertia is valuable only when paired with intelligent design.* A poorly constructed portfolio left unattended is neglect, not discipline. But a well-constructed one allowed to operate freely is the apex of intelligent investing. The investor's job is not to steer endlessly, but to set the correct initial path and then minimise interference.

Modern investing, unfortunately, is full of noise that disrupts this stillness. Real-time price updates, sensationalist headlines, and platforms that make trading feel like gaming—all conspire against inertia. They create artificial reasons to act. And every action—no matter how logical it seems at the time—breaks the motion. The investor pays for it not only in pounds and pence, but in attention and energy. These are not trivial losses. They erode the very quality that compounding demands above all else: patience.

Even seasoned professionals fall into this trap. Hedge fund managers, who are paid handsomely to outperform, often trade so actively that their performance is eclipsed by index trackers. According to S&P's SPIVA data, most actively managed funds underperform their benchmarks over time. This is not because the managers lack intelligence. It's because constant action introduces too much friction. Markets are complex systems, not puzzles to be solved with more effort. At scale, inertia often beats ingenuity.

There is a lesson here that transcends finance. Systems—biological, mechanical, psychological—perform better when designed to operate with minimal interference. An ecosystem flourishes not through daily adjustment but through structural balance. A machine runs smoothly when lubricated and left to perform its function without tampering. A mind, too, often thinks more clearly when not flooded with constant stimulus. The principle is universal: once a system is working, disturbance is more likely to harm than help.

For the investor, this principle must be operationalised. That means reducing the number of inputs that lead to action. It means automating contributions, limiting portfolio checks, and writing investment policies that define *when* action is permitted and *why*. It means seeing markets through the lens of decades, not days. And it means trusting that a well-structured portfolio—like a body in motion—will, over time, get to where it is going, provided it is not disturbed.

The psychology of inertia is perhaps its most challenging aspect. To do nothing while others act—especially in volatile markets—requires more than patience. It requires identity-level conviction. It means seeing yourself not as a market participant in a daily game, but as an architect of long-range systems. This reframing is what separates noise-chasers from builders. The latter understand that success is not won in real-time; it is accrued silently, over years of sustained motion.

And so, to praise inertia is not to glorify laziness. It is to elevate *disciplined stillness*. It is to recognise that in a market system filled with activity, the greatest returns accrue not to those who move fastest, but to those who move least—strategically, sparingly, and with conviction. Money, like matter, moves best when left alone—if, and only if, its motion was intelligently initiated. The work is in the design. The reward is in the stillness that follows.

The Enemy Is the Tweak

The most costly decisions in investing are rarely catastrophic errors. They're the small, subtle, well-intentioned adjustments—the tweaks. They come disguised as prudence, framed as optimisation, often made by smart people with good intentions. A 5% shift toward a "hot" sector. A minor reallocation in response to market chatter. A revised weighting based on new data. None of these decisions feel reckless in the moment. But over time, they accumulate into a pattern that quietly erodes the very edge long-term investors rely on: consistency. In investing, *the enemy is not dramatic failure—it's the erosion of a working system through constant fine-tuning.*

To appreciate the scale of this problem, one must begin by understanding the psychology of control. Investors often view their portfolio as something that should reflect their current thinking. But markets do not reward novelty. They reward patience. When you construct a portfolio with a sound design—appropriate asset allocation, time horizon alignment, and diversification—the most productive decision is often to *leave it alone*. The temptation to adjust it frequently stems not from logic but from discomfort. Discomfort with uncertainty, with underperformance, with boredom. In this way, tweaking becomes a psychological reflex, not a strategic act.

Take, for example, the case of a high-earning professional—an experienced engineer in her late 40s—who had built a sensible, globally diversified ETF-based portfolio in the early 2010s. After reading about the "rise of emerging markets," she gradually increased her EM exposure from 15% to nearly 40% of her equity allocation over a span of three years. It didn't feel impulsive at the time; each move was small, spaced out, and backed by articles and economic outlooks. But the result was severe underperformance relative to a simple global equity tracker over the next half-decade. Her tweak didn't just fail—it *muted* the compounding of her original strategy. Not because her logic was flawed, but because her system lost its integrity.

This is the essential insight: *tweaks dilute coherence.* Each adjustment, no matter how slight, introduces new dependencies into a system. If you tilt toward technology stocks, you're now not just betting on markets—you're betting on sector dominance. If you reduce bonds because interest rates "might" rise, you've converted a diversified allocation into a rate call. These are no longer passive portfolios. They are active expressions of conviction, whether the investor acknowledges it or not. And active bets require a standard of insight most investors simply don't possess—nor need to.

Even institutional investors aren't immune. A study published by the National Bureau of Economic Research analysed the allocation changes of large U.S. pension funds. It found that frequent reallocation—especially in response to recent performance—resulted in lower long-term returns than a simple fixed-allocation strategy. Pension boards, seeking to "fine-tune" their exposures based on macro forecasts, ended up selling winners and buying underperformers at precisely the wrong times. These weren't emotional amateurs—they were fiduciaries with access to top-tier research. And still, the tweaks did more harm than good.

Why is tweaking so seductive? Because it offers the illusion of engagement without the cost of overhaul. It lets the investor feel involved, decisive, and proactive. But engagement, in investing, is a double-edged sword. When it's misdirected—when it manifests as continual revision rather than initial precision—it becomes corrosive. The portfolio becomes a mirror of short-term thinking rather than long-term design.

This is where the concept of *design inertia* becomes essential. A well-structured portfolio should function like a well-designed machine: capable of running with minimal interference. Engineers do not tinker with turbines mid-flight. Surgeons do not rewire machines mid-operation. And yet investors, operating with less precision and more emotion, feel compelled to continuously adjust a system already built to withstand volatility. The problem isn't ignorance—it's restlessness.

This restlessness is amplified by the architecture of the investing environment. Online platforms allow for real-time rebalancing. News feeds continually flag "opportunities." Financial media incentivises forecasts over silence. The entire ecosystem is designed to provoke response. In such a landscape, the absence of action feels like negligence. But it is precisely this misperception that the disciplined investor must overcome. *Stillness is not negligence—it is mastery over unnecessary motion.*

Consider also the role of comparative anxiety. Investors rarely evaluate their portfolios in isolation. They compare. To friends, to benchmarks, to last year's performance. When a colleague's speculative bet pays off, the temptation to tweak one's own allocations rises—not because of market fundamentals, but because of social discomfort. Performance envy is one of the least discussed but most powerful triggers for unforced errors. It turns calm investors into tinkerers.

The cost of these tweaks is measurable. According to DALBAR's widely cited Quantitative Analysis of Investor Behavior, the average equity mutual fund investor has underperformed the market by several percentage points annually over the last 20 years. While fees and poor timing explain some of the gap, frequent reallocation—triggered by short-term sentiment and external signals—is a major culprit. It's not that investors lack access to good strategies. It's that they fail to *stay inside them.*

There is a subtle but important distinction between *rebalancing* and tweaking. Rebalancing is rule-based. It's part of the original design. It follows a predetermined rhythm or threshold, and it exists to preserve allocation integrity. Tweaking, on the other hand, is reactive. It's discretionary. It happens because something "feels off" or "looks promising." Rebalancing maintains the machine. Tweaking modifies the blueprint. One supports discipline; the other indulges uncertainty.

The antidote to tweaking is not paralysis—it is clarity. Clarity about what the portfolio is designed to do. Clarity about the time horizon it must serve. Clarity about the kinds of market behaviour it is meant to endure. When these variables are explicit, the need for constant adjustment diminishes. The investor understands that short-term underperformance is not failure. It is the expected cost of a strategy playing out over a long arc.

This understanding must also extend to self-awareness. Investors must recognise the internal cues that trigger the impulse to tweak. Is it fear? Is it boredom? Is it discomfort with non-action? These are not weaknesses to be ashamed of. They are simply signals to be acknowledged. But acknowledging them is not the same as obeying them.

To mature as an investor is to develop the capacity to *let a good system run.* To trust that enough has been built into the design, and that doing more will likely achieve less. It is a shift in focus—from action to architecture, from performance to durability.

Tweaking will always feel tempting. It flatters the intellect and soothes the ego. But when it becomes habitual, it destroys the very advantage the long-term investor possesses: alignment with time. The longer your money compounds uninterrupted, the more powerful it becomes. That power does not need your constant help. It needs your thoughtful absence.

A portfolio is not a pet to be fussed over. It is a mechanism, built to operate through seasons, shocks, and silence. The enemy is not volatility, underperformance, or even loss. The enemy is the compulsion to adjust what already works. The tweak may feel like control—but more often, it is the interruption of something that was working better than you realised.

Letting Systems Breathe

There's an enduring paradox in personal finance: the more you engineer your portfolio to run without you, the more reliably it builds wealth. And yet, for many investors—especially intelligent, ambitious ones—this idea feels deeply counterintuitive. We are taught that success is the product of effort, vigilance, and iteration. In most domains, that's true. A surgeon improves with each procedure. A writer sharpens with each draft. A business grows with sustained strategic input. But investing is different. Once a sound financial system is designed, the optimal intervention is often none at all. The problem isn't laziness. The problem is that we haven't been taught how to *design for absence.*

Letting systems breathe is not about detachment or indifference. It's about architecture—creating a structure robust enough to operate independently of constant oversight. In investing, this means crafting portfolios and processes that function effectively whether or not you're paying attention. The value of such a design isn't just found in financial returns, but in reduced decision fatigue, lower emotional volatility, and the liberation of time. It is the clearest path to what the disciplined investor ultimately seeks: not just wealth, but *peace of mind.*

To understand the power of this approach, it helps to observe those who've done it successfully. Take, for instance, Ronald Read—a Vermont janitor and gas station attendant who died in 2014 with an estate worth over $8 million. Read didn't win the lottery, inherit money, or run a side business. He invested consistently in high-quality dividend-paying stocks, reinvested the proceeds, and left his portfolio alone. For decades. What allowed his wealth to compound wasn't genius stock-picking or active portfolio management. It was time, structure, and the absence of interference. Read didn't supervise his system daily. He let it breathe.

Contrast that with the behaviour of many high-income professionals, who, despite access to research, data, and capital, often underperform basic market indices. Why? Because their portfolios require constant oversight. They build strategies that are sophisticated in theory but fragile in practice. They attempt to hedge every scenario, time every market shift, and fine-tune every allocation. These systems aren't resilient. They're reactive. And because they demand attention, they frequently invite it—even when attention becomes a liability.

The problem isn't just tactical—it's philosophical. Investors often conflate intelligence with intervention. They believe that being smarter means seeing around corners, and that insight must always be applied. But what if the real test of intelligence in investing is the ability to *not act*? What if wisdom lies not in anticipating every scenario, but in designing a portfolio that doesn't require you to?

This is where the concept of *anti-fragility* becomes especially useful. An anti-fragile system doesn't merely survive volatility; it benefits from it. Portfolios that are built with simplicity, diversification, and long-term time horizons—augmented by regular, rule-based rebalancing—tend to perform better not because they predict the future, but because they *accommodate* it. These systems can absorb shocks, adjust automatically, and continue compounding while the investor steps away. That's not neglect. It's intentional robustness.

To build such a system requires three core principles: structural clarity, behavioural insulation, and rule-based automation. Structural clarity means knowing exactly what your portfolio is built to do. Are you investing for retirement in 30 years? For homeownership in five? For intergenerational transfer? Each goal requires a different design. Without that clarity, portfolios become vague reflections of fear, hope, and hunches—far too reliant on day-to-day inputs.

Behavioural insulation is what protects the system from its creator. It means creating buffers between your emotions and your portfolio. This might take the form of pre-set rebalancing schedules, limited account access, or delegated management. It may mean using automated investing platforms that restrict ad hoc adjustments. The objective is not to reduce intelligence, but to *outsource impulse control.* You are designing for your future self—not the calm version reading this book, but the stressed one reacting to a market correction on a Tuesday afternoon.

Rule-based automation is the operational engine. It converts intentions into protocol. This can include automatic contributions tied to income, target allocations that rebalance when thresholds are crossed, and withdrawal strategies that adjust based on market conditions. These rules need not be complex. In fact, simpler systems are usually more durable. But they must be designed *before* the emotion arrives. That's when good investing becomes behavioural engineering.

Let's be clear: letting systems breathe is not about embracing a one-size-fits-all, set-it-and-forget-it dogma. It's about distinguishing between *initial design* and *ongoing maintenance.* The former requires creativity, critical thinking, and thoughtful planning. The latter should require as little of you as possible. An intelligent investor designs once—and designs well. What follows is stewardship, not supervision.

Consider the case of index investing. It's often dismissed as simplistic or unambitious. But many of the wealthiest families, endowments, and foundations rely heavily on passive strategies—not because they lack access to complex tools, but because they understand the cost of complexity. Jack Bogle, the late founder of

Vanguard, once said, "Don't do something. Just stand there." He wasn't advocating paralysis. He was endorsing design integrity—the ability to trust a system built on sound principles and leave it alone long enough to perform.

The financial services industry often resists this message. Not because it's wrong, but because it's unprofitable. Portfolios that don't need supervision don't generate commissions. Strategies that don't require ongoing advice don't justify annual fees. This is why so much of the industry is built around activity—new products, rebalancing reports, tactical shifts. Letting systems breathe doesn't sell. But it builds wealth.

There is also a cultural dimension. In a world that glorifies hustle and responsiveness, *deliberate disengagement* looks suspect. Investors are praised for their savvy moves, not for their refusal to make them. A system that operates invisibly, quietly compounding in the background, lacks theatre. But wealth doesn't need theatre. It needs time, discipline, and the humility to step back.

We must reframe what it means to be a "good investor." It's not the person who checks the market daily, reads every economic outlook, or rotates their portfolio quarterly. It's the person who builds a system that continues working whether or not they show up. This isn't laziness. It's design maturity. It recognises that the most valuable financial strategies are the ones that require the least management, not because they're perfect, but because they're built to withstand imperfection.

There's a simple test: *What would happen to your portfolio if you went offline for a year?* Would it continue to allocate automatically? Would contributions continue? Would it rebalance within defined tolerances? Would your plan remain intact? If not, the system doesn't serve you—you serve it. The goal is not to micromanage your wealth. It's to structure it so effectively that your primary job is not to act, but to *stay out of its way.*

Letting systems breathe is an act of restraint and foresight. It is the practical application of respect for time, discipline, and compound growth. In a field dominated by noise, it is the rarest and most underrated signal. The investor who learns to build systems that don't need them discovers something most of the market never will: that success often looks like silence, feels like stillness, and functions best when it is quietly doing its work—without you.

From Micro-Managing to Macro-Mapping

One of the most destructive habits in investing—particularly among intelligent, high-functioning individuals—is the compulsion to manage things too closely. Not recklessly. Not dramatically. But constantly. Every market update feels like a referendum. Every news headline triggers an analysis. Every minor dip tempts a decision. This pattern doesn't always look chaotic. In fact, it often masquerades as discipline. But in the long-term architecture of wealth, *over-management is not discipline—it's drift.* It pulls the investor's focus downward and inward, from structural strategy to short-term noise, from long-range intention to daily interpretation. The result is distraction disguised as engagement.

To counteract this behavioural drift, the investor must undergo a mental shift—a reorientation from micro-managing toward *macro-mapping.* It's not a rejection of data or diligence. It's a re-scaling of time. A move from the immediacy of the moment to the endurance of decades. Most importantly, it's a refusal to be drawn into the theatre of now. And at the centre of this shift lies a powerful and deceptively simple tool: the *decade filter.*

The decade filter is a question, but also a mental framework. It asks: *Will this decision still make sense ten years from today?* Not ten days. Not ten months. Ten years. This filter, when applied consistently, rewires an investor's cognitive habits. It shifts the axis of relevance. Suddenly, earnings reports, market cycles, election headlines, and asset class fads lose their urgency. They don't disappear—but they are reframed. You are no longer asking what's happening now, but whether what's happening now matters at all in the context of enduring growth.

This is not abstract theory. In practice, long-term thinking is what separates those who accumulate wealth from those who chase it. Take the case of Warren Buffett, whose most powerful investing skill is not his stock-picking, but his timeline. He holds companies for decades, often enduring years of underperformance. Why? Because the systems he builds are judged on ten-year arcs, not quarterly snapshots. Or consider the Norwegian Sovereign Wealth Fund—one of the largest and most successful in the world—which publishes strategy papers detailing hundred-year outlooks. Their asset allocation, risk tolerance, and withdrawal rates are all structured not around current conditions, but multi-decade design. That's macro-mapping in action.

By contrast, most individual investors—even sophisticated ones—operate on a time horizon that shrinks during volatility. A plan that felt stable at the start of the year feels suspect by August. A market correction triggers not analysis, but anxiety. The result? Tinkering. Allocation changes. Hedging. Switching to cash. These are not errors in judgement—they are errors in timeframe. The investor believes they're being responsive. In reality, they're abandoning the map.

There's a psychological nuance here worth exploring. When you think in decades, you automatically shrink the emotional significance of today. You start to notice how often the market recovers, how rarely "this time is different" truly is, and how consistently patience is rewarded—not with perfection, but with power. More importantly, you become harder to provoke. And in investing, *emotional provocation is the enemy of compounding.*

But adopting the decade filter isn't just about resisting panic. It's also about resisting performance obsession. Many investors, particularly those who are used to excelling in other areas of life, approach markets with the expectation that effort will yield outperformance.

They become portfolio micromanagers, adjusting for perceived inefficiencies, reading constantly, rotating between sectors. But as decades of data show, frequent intervention almost always diminishes returns—especially after costs, taxes, and timing errors are accounted for. The irony is that those who treat investing as a constant project usually underperform those who treat it as a strategic infrastructure to be maintained, not manipulated.

Macro-mapping asks something difficult but essential: that you focus less on what your portfolio is doing *today*, and more on whether it's positioned to do what it needs to *eventually*. That means building a plan rooted in long-term purpose—retirement income, intergenerational transfer, lifestyle independence—and then reverse-engineering the portfolio from that objective. It is architecture, not reaction. The map is not a forecast. It is a design that accommodates uncertainty without requiring constant rerouting.

There is another benefit to this mindset shift: it clarifies what matters. When you evaluate decisions through the lens of a decade, much of what dominates financial media becomes irrelevant. Will today's inflation print matter in 2034? Will the outcome of this quarter's GDP report shape your life in a meaningful way ten years from now? If not, then it need not drive your behaviour. The decade filter doesn't suppress curiosity—it filters signal from noise. It makes space for the investor to stop reacting and start building.

And what does building look like under this framework? It looks like committing to a target allocation and sticking to it unless your life circumstances—not your feelings—have changed. It looks like automating contributions, reducing portfolio checks, and measuring success in terms of *alignment with plan*, not performance versus peers. It looks like viewing volatility not as a problem to be solved, but a condition to be endured—and priced into your original design.

The best investors are not those who anticipate every twist in the economic narrative. They are those who ask, again and again: *What does this decision look like on a 10-year chart?* If the answer is unclear, the decision is probably unnecessary. If the answer is sound, it doesn't need to be re-justified every week.

This is not about being inert. Macro-mapping does not mean ignoring changes in life, income, goals, or family dynamics. It means building a framework that can absorb and adapt to those changes without needing constant handholding. It means shifting from a day-to-day user of markets to a long-term architect of your financial ecosystem.

The temptation to micromanage will always exist. The markets will never stop moving. The headlines will never stop shouting. But the investor who shifts perspective—from the immediate to the essential, from micro-managing to macro-mapping—discovers a kind of calm that cannot be bought, timed, or sold. It is earned through clarity, through consistency, and through the courage to think in decades.

The decade filter is not a tactic. It is a philosophy of scale and patience. It invites the investor to move beyond the horizon of the urgent and into the quiet terrain where wealth is truly built—not through noise, but through structure. Not through reaction, but through design. And once that design is in place, the smartest thing you can do is let it lead, and get out of its way.

Chapter 3
The Emotional Dividend Curve

Markets move in cycles. Portfolios compound with time. Wealth, when left uninterrupted, tends to expand. Most investors accept these truths intellectually, yet the human psyche rarely follows the same predictable rhythm. Volatility exists not only in asset prices but within the nervous systems of those managing them. Exposure to risk is one thing; exposure to the perception of risk is far more unpredictable—and often far more punishing. The paradox of modern investing is stark: net worth may climb while anxiety escalates. Financial resilience quietly accumulates, yet emotional fragility can intensify. This chapter addresses that dissonance, exploring why some investors grow richer yet simultaneously more uneasy, and how to recalibrate the relationship between money and mental clarity.

Central to this discussion is what we call the emotional dividend curve—a map, not of financial accumulation, but of psychological trajectory. In theory, compounding ought to reassure: more assets, greater buffers, expanded freedom. In practice, it often brings increased monitoring, amplified stress, and heightened perception of exposure. Wealth transforms from a shield into a stimulus for vigilance. Instead of savouring the slope of the curve, investors become trapped in perpetual "what if" cycles, a phenomenon that might be described as prosperity dysphoria: abundance paired with uncertainty.

This tension is not confined to novices. It intensifies the more there is to lose. A financial adviser I interviewed recounted a recurring pattern among high-net-worth clients: the wealthier they became, the more their behaviour betrayed scarcity thinking. Accounts were checked multiple times daily. Market dips triggered obsessive monitoring. Articles on inflation, taxation, currency risk, and geopolitical upheaval were devoured—often far beyond their tangible exposure. These were rational, educated, even entrepreneurial individuals. Yet emotionally, they were suspended in a state of hyper-vigilance. Portfolios matured; psychology lagged behind.

The distinction between financial resilience and emotional satisfaction is pivotal. Many assume that a certain net worth automatically begets peace of mind. It does not. One can be secure on paper while fragile in spirit. This is particularly visible among first-generation wealth creators who internalised scarcity in childhood. Their monitoring, over-hedging, and reactive behaviours are not strategy—they are the residue of survival instincts. Even those without such a history are vulnerable in today's hyper-visible finance culture.

Modern investing fosters compulsive engagement. Markets reside perpetually in our pockets. In moments, investors can track every asset, compare themselves with peers, or absorb hours of commentary. This accessibility masquerades as empowerment, but often functions more like addiction. The cost is not merely temporal; it is cognitive. Each refresh triggers a micro-assessment: Am I ahead? Am I safe? Should I act? The cadence of long-term investing is replaced by incessant, short-term self-evaluation, breaking natural rhythms and embedding emotional tethering to performance.

Cognitive science explains the effect. Brains are wired to prioritise immediate feedback, not probabilistic abstraction. Red numbers do not register as future opportunity—they register as threat, activating stress responses. Repeated exposure reinforces this conditioning. Investors transition from owners to gamblers, scanning compulsively, emotionally hostage to fluctuations, no longer confident in the systems they themselves built.

Here the blindfold metaphor becomes useful—not as ignorance, but as intentional disengagement. Once a robust system exists, step back. Not permanently, but sufficiently to detach psychology from the minutiae of market noise. Blindfold yourself, not in unawareness, but in trust. Let the mechanism operate undisturbed. This is not avoidance of knowledge but a prioritisation: focus on what informs productive action, not on what triggers compulsion.

We are taught that more knowledge drives better outcomes. In investing, this principle falters. Beyond a certain point, additional input produces noise, not insight. Behavioural finance repeatedly confirms that frequent monitoring correlates with lower satisfaction and, often, inferior results. Skill is not lacking; strategy is hijacked by volatility rather than value.

How, then, to reverse this dynamic? The shift begins by redefining richness—not as a ledger of numbers, but as a subjective state of adequacy, autonomy, and calm. To "feel rich, think lazy" is to cultivate a mindset where wealth functions as a platform, not a performance. The goal is to construct a portfolio that allows the investor to forget it exists for most of the year, not because of indifference, but because design and automation are sufficient. Feeling rich emerges from trust, not observation.

Practical measures—automation, diversification, scheduled rebalancing—support this reframing. Yet without an aligned mindset, tools are impotent. One can automate and still obsess. Diversify and still feel fragile. Outer systems matter; inner systems determine experience. Redefining success emotionally is essential; otherwise, wealth remains performance-chained, never truly experienced.

This chapter therefore examines more than financial mechanics. It explores the anatomy of financial anxiety, the hidden cost of over-information, and the liberating effects of deliberate stillness. It teaches how to separate the sensation of wealth from its visible markers and design strategies that preserve calm while compounding capital. Over time, the greatest dividend is not measured in percentages—it is measured in peace.

In the pages ahead, we explore anxiety's architecture, the pitfalls of hyper-vigilance, and the transformative power of a lazy, intentional approach. The emotional dividend curve need not invert. With structure, clarity, and disciplined disengagement, investors can grow both wealth and composure—provided they relinquish constant control and invest with confidence as well as capital.

Why Anxiety Outpaces Returns

An investment portfolio can double in a decade, yet an investor's anxiety can triple in a week. This is the paradox at the heart of modern wealth-building: while financial assets often grow predictably over time, emotional distress can escalate faster than returns—especially for those who remain tethered to daily outcomes. Markets reward patience, structure, and time. Human psychology, on the other hand, often rewards none of those things. Without a deliberate effort to create emotional distance, wealth accumulation becomes less about performance and more about endurance—*not of volatility, but of vigilance.*

For all the attention given to risk management, portfolio theory, and diversification, relatively little is said about the *psychological yield curve*—the way mental and emotional states evolve as capital grows. The assumption is that more wealth leads to more security. But this correlation often breaks down in practice. Emotional discomfort does not scale linearly with portfolio growth. It often intensifies. Investors become more aware of their exposure, more alert to market movements, and more preoccupied with maintaining gains than they ever were with building them. Fear does not recede with affluence; it mutates.

A compelling example comes from a client of a major private bank—an entrepreneur who had recently sold his business for just under £20 million. Despite now being in the top 0.1% of wealth holders, he experienced near-daily panic about market downturns. He had more than enough to live comfortably for the rest of his life. Yet he would call his adviser multiple times per week, asking if they should move everything to cash, or buy gold, or hedge against political unrest. The bank had modelled his risk capacity to be high. But his *risk tolerance*—the emotional ability to live with uncertainty—was low. The portfolio was fine. The owner was not.

This kind of anxiety is not merely unfortunate. It's corrosive. Financial hyper-vigilance has real psychological costs. It creates a state of persistent low-grade stress that depletes attention, sleep quality, and even physical health. It reduces one's ability to enjoy the fruits of their labour. More subtly, it reshapes an investor's relationship to time. When anxiety takes over, the investment horizon collapses. The future becomes a threat, not a promise. The investor begins to scan for danger, not for opportunity. And the entire premise of long-term growth—letting time do the compounding—becomes emotionally untenable.

This isn't just anecdotal. Research in behavioural finance confirms that emotional reactivity often *outpaces* portfolio risk. A 2022 paper in the *Journal of Financial Planning* found that investors who checked their accounts more than once a day reported lower financial satisfaction, even when their portfolios were performing well. Another study, led by Professor Meir Statman of Santa Clara University, demonstrated that emotional loss aversion was often more influenced by *recent checking behaviour* than by actual market declines. The act of monitoring created the perception of loss, even when no transaction had occurred.

This cognitive distortion is compounded by what psychologists call *availability bias*: the tendency to overweight information that is most readily accessible. When investors surround themselves with daily price updates, real-time volatility becomes the dominant mental narrative. The mind starts to interpret market noise as meaning. And meaning demands action. This sets off a dangerous loop: more monitoring leads to more emotional reactivity, which leads to more portfolio meddling, which leads—more often than not—to underperformance. The investor is not responding to the market. They are responding to *how often they see the market.*

Contrast this with the behaviour of those who insulate themselves from unnecessary data. In one informal study by a U.S. brokerage firm, clients who had forgotten their accounts—literally lost access and didn't log in for years—outperformed more active investors. Why? Because they never interrupted the curve. They let their system operate without interference. Their returns weren't just financial. They were psychological. They experienced none of the mental friction that erodes satisfaction, weakens confidence, and leads to overreaction.

Of course, ignoring your investments completely is not a solution. But it does raise a critical question: *how much exposure to your portfolio is psychologically optimal?* At what point does attentiveness turn into harm? There is no universal answer, but the direction of travel is clear. Most investors benefit not from more data, but from better filters. They don't need to know *more*, but to engage *less frequently and more meaningfully*.

This is where the idea of *psychological detachment* becomes essential. It's not about caring less. It's about *caring differently*. It's about understanding that emotional engagement must be structured just as deliberately as asset allocation. Left unmanaged, your attention becomes the most volatile asset in the portfolio. To detach is to place boundaries between what the system is designed to do, and what your brain is wired to want: immediate resolution.

The emotional cost of hyper-vigilance is also relational. It seeps into how investors talk about money, how they view others, how they allocate time. A wealth holder who is in a state of constant alertness may become less generous, less trusting, and less present in non-financial domains of life. Their identity begins to revolve around control. Not just of capital, but of uncertainty itself. And this is a losing battle. Markets are not tameable. They are not puzzles to be solved with enough information. They are adaptive systems. The only control that works is structural. Everything else is noise management.

One of the most dangerous myths in modern investing is that anxiety is the price of vigilance. That to be on top of things is to be forever uneasy. But the truth is more nuanced. *Real vigilance is quiet.* It's built into systems, not stress levels. It's embedded in rebalancing schedules, contribution plans, and withdrawal strategies—not in constant monitoring or speculative reaction.

The investor must learn to *separate perceived risk from real risk*. Perceived risk is what you feel after reading ten headlines in a row. Real risk is what happens when you deviate from a strategy built for your actual life needs. Perceived risk can make you act urgently. Real risk usually arrives slowly—when a poorly thought-out change compounds over time. Knowing the difference between the two is a kind of emotional literacy. It protects you from confusing fear with information.

So how does one begin to reverse the trend—so that emotional calm compounds at the same pace as financial capital? It starts with redefining what success feels like. If every gain is shadowed by the fear of losing it, if every market movement is interpreted as a threat, then growth becomes psychologically expensive. It demands more from you than it gives. But when you build a system that allows you to *experience wealth with distance*, something shifts. You begin to measure success not just in balance sheets, but in *mental spaciousness*.

The irony is that many investors already have the portfolios they need. What they lack is a way to relate to those portfolios that doesn't feel like a fight. The next frontier of wealth building is not smarter trades. It's quieter minds. Minds that can hold volatility without flinching. Minds that have designed for noise, and no longer confuse movement with meaning. Minds that understand the markets will rise, fall, recover—and that the greatest returns are those you feel internally, not just those that show up on a spreadsheet.

To build wealth is one thing. To hold it without holding your breath—that's something rarer. Something quieter. And far more powerful.

Satisfaction vs. Security

A person can be worth £10 million and still feel financially unsafe. Another, with modest savings and a paid-off home, may sleep soundly each night, free of monetary worry. These contrasting states reveal a simple but overlooked truth in personal finance: *wealth is not synonymous with security*, and *security is not synonymous with satisfaction*. The financial industry tends to conflate these dimensions, offering products and advice as if emotional peace were the inevitable by-product of portfolio construction. It is not. Emotional satisfaction with money is psychological. Financial resilience is structural. One can exist without the other—and frequently does.

We have been taught to equate more with safer, to assume that a higher net worth equals lower vulnerability. But the reality is more complex. There is a phenomenon among the affluent—particularly self-made wealth holders—of living with a near-constant undercurrent of worry. Call it *high-net-worry syndrome.* These individuals have objectively strong balance sheets, yet remain preoccupied with "what if" scenarios, market volatility, tax policy changes, or the fear that they might someday need more than they have.

Consider the case of a London-based technology founder who, after selling his company for £42 million, commissioned a comprehensive financial plan. His assets were allocated across private equity, commercial real estate, index funds, and bonds. By every measure—liquidity, diversification, inflation hedging—he was secure. Yet he admitted to checking the FTSE, S&P, and his private dashboards multiple times per day. He reported trouble sleeping during market downturns, despite knowing rationally that his core capital was largely unexposed. His worry was not about reality. It was about perception—about what might happen to his *sense* of being secure, not his actual security.

This mental dislocation isn't rare. A study by UBS on high-net-worth investors found that nearly 60% of individuals with over £5 million in assets feared running out of money during retirement. What makes this even more striking is that their financial advisers often calculated their risk of depleting assets at below 2%. That is, the *maths* says they're safe. But their *minds* say otherwise. This dissonance reveals a core problem in how we understand and pursue financial peace: we think it is a function of net worth, but it is actually a function of narrative.

Satisfaction with wealth is deeply narrative-dependent. It comes less from the number of digits in a bank account and more from the meaning we assign to those digits. Does the capital represent autonomy or obligation? Does it fuel a sense of freedom or invite fear of loss? Satisfaction arises when our internal story aligns with our external structure—when how we feel about our money matches what the money is actually doing. Without this alignment, even perfect planning can feel like peril.

Security, by contrast, is measurable. It involves asset-liability matching, liquidity reserves, income diversification, tax efficiency, and time horizon integrity. It is built through deliberate, system-level design. Satisfaction, however, is *felt*, not engineered. It often lags behind wealth creation. People don't suddenly become more serene when their net worth crosses a threshold. In many cases, emotional distress *increases* with net worth, because more wealth introduces more complexity, more choice, and more potential points of perceived failure.

To bridge this gap, we must first recognise that *feeling secure and being secure are two separate skills.* The former is emotional regulation; the latter is structural architecture. Conflating the two creates blind spots in both directions. Some investors over-engineer for control, mistaking vigilance for resilience. Others assume emotional calm means they're covered, ignoring the need for systems that actually hold up under strain. The mature investor must develop both: a resilient portfolio and a disciplined mind.

One illuminating case involved a couple in their late forties, both executives at multinational firms. They had accumulated a combined net worth of approximately £8 million, including pensions, property, and investments. Their adviser had stress-tested every major scenario—health events, job loss, early retirement—and confirmed they were on solid footing. Yet they expressed chronic anxiety over whether their two children would be "OK" financially. They regularly moved investments based on geopolitical events, even when those events had little bearing on their long-term plan. Their fear, it turned out, was not about the numbers. It was about *control.* They were trying to engineer certainty in a world that doesn't offer it.

This reflex—to seek control when uncertainty feels threatening—is biologically encoded. Neuroscience has shown that the brain interprets uncertainty as a threat, activating the same stress pathways as physical danger. In this state, people overestimate risks and undervalue long-term thinking. They look for actions—any actions—that create the *illusion* of control. This can take the form of excessive monitoring, frequent rebalancing, speculative hedging, or simply obsessing over "what if" scenarios. The activity feels productive. But it rarely is.

This is where the concept of *emotional financial planning* becomes critical. Traditional financial planning is objective: What do you have? What do you need? What's the delta? Emotional financial planning asks different questions: How do you feel about what you have? What do you fear losing? What are you trying to protect—your assets, or your identity? These questions are uncomfortable. But they are necessary. Because until you answer them, no structure will feel sufficient.

This brings us to a simple but powerful insight: *satisfaction comes from coherence between plan and purpose.* If you've built a portfolio that matches your values and your real-life needs, then you don't need to check it constantly to feel okay. But if your investment strategy is disconnected from your psychology, even a well-performing portfolio can feel like a source of stress. Satisfaction, then, is not an outcome of market performance—it is a by-product of internal alignment.

Consider the framework used by a Scandinavian family office that advises generational wealth holders. Before any investment is made, clients are asked to write a "statement of financial purpose"—a brief narrative explaining what their capital is *for*, beyond returns. This exercise, seemingly simple, shifts focus from accumulation to application. One client, a third-generation heir, wrote that his wealth existed to fund education and protect his family's independence. This clarity allowed him to tune out market noise and focus on cash flow sustainability rather than beating benchmarks. His sense of security came not from having "enough," but from knowing why he had it.

This example illustrates a broader principle: *satisfaction is not found at the end of a growth curve.* It emerges when money is put in service of something meaningful, and when that meaning is stable enough to withstand short-term fluctuations. Most investors don't need more capital. They need more clarity. They need a way to interpret their wealth that doesn't make them its prisoner.

It is worth noting that satisfaction does not require ignorance. It doesn't mean you stop learning, adapting, or being prudent. It means you stop mistaking *more information* for *more security*. It means designing an investment life that generates peace, not just returns. The irony is that many of the behaviours associated with risk mitigation—frequent checking, obsessive analysis, tactical reallocations—often *increase* emotional fragility. True financial resilience is not just about surviving downturns. It's about remaining internally calm while doing so.

The investor who understands this begins to relate to their capital differently. They stop asking, "Do I have enough?" and start asking, "Does what I have support the life I want to live?" That shift reframes everything—from portfolio design to time allocation. It invites a more humane relationship with money, one in which the metrics of success are emotional, not just numerical.

To feel safe with your wealth is not a privilege reserved for the ultra-rich. It is a discipline—a form of financial maturity that can be cultivated at any level. But it requires a refusal to outsource peace of mind to market performance. It requires seeing that satisfaction is not a passive outcome of financial success. It is a skill. And like any skill, it can be learned, strengthened, and—perhaps most importantly—practised in silence.

The Cost of Checking

It starts innocently. A glance at your portfolio app while waiting for your morning coffee. A quick scan of the market indices during a lull in a meeting. An end-of-day scroll through headlines about tech stocks, interest rates, and "expert" predictions. These micro-checks, which feel harmless and even productive in the moment, are costing far more than they seem—not just in time and attention, but in clarity, confidence, and long-term financial performance. Frequent portfolio checking is the most socially accepted form of financial self-sabotage. It cloaks itself as responsibility, but behaves like addiction.

The paradox is striking: as technology has made portfolio visibility effortless, investor behaviour has become more reactive and less rational. Today's investors can monitor every tick in the market from the palm of their hand—yet emotional peace has plummeted. Access has increased, and satisfaction has decreased. This is not a coincidence. It is the psychological tax of hyper-awareness. The more frequently you monitor your investments, the more volatility you perceive, and the more volatility you perceive, the more risk you *feel*—even when no risk has materially changed.

Behavioural finance research confirms what many intuitively suspect: *the more often you look, the worse things appear.* This isn't just a subjective feeling. Studies have shown that investors who check their portfolios daily perceive losses more often than gains, even when the market is generally trending upward. This is a direct result of how markets behave in the short term. On a day-to-day basis, price movements are mostly noise—random, shallow fluctuations driven by sentiment, liquidity, or news cycles. But psychologically, losses loom larger than gains, a phenomenon known as *loss aversion.* The result is that frequent monitoring disproportionately exposes investors to perceived losses, which fuels anxiety and triggers premature or unnecessary intervention.

A 1997 study by Shlomo Benartzi and Richard Thaler coined the term *myopic loss aversion* to describe this phenomenon. The researchers found that when people evaluated their investments infrequently—say, once a year—they were far more likely to stick with sound long-term strategies. But when returns were shown on a more frequent basis, tolerance for risk decreased sharply. Simply put: *looking more often made people feel worse, even when the data hadn't changed.* This tendency leads not only to emotional wear, but also to behavioural drift—reactive decisions that reduce the probability of meeting long-term goals.

Real-world examples bear this out. Consider the case of an investor with a globally diversified equity portfolio. During the COVID-19 market shock of March 2020, they began checking their portfolio multiple times a day. Despite understanding that their time horizon was decades—not months—they moved a large portion of their holdings into cash after watching several days of red screens. Within weeks, markets rebounded dramatically. By the time this investor re-entered, they had missed the sharpest recovery in modern financial history. The loss was not in the portfolio. It was in the behaviour. And the behaviour was triggered by *over-monitoring.*

Frequent checking doesn't only impair judgement—it distorts it. It narrows your perspective to daily movements, rather than systemic outcomes. It exaggerates the significance of small fluctuations and downplays the power of long-term compounding. More dangerously, it increases your susceptibility to *narrative volatility.* When you monitor too frequently, you're not just seeing numbers—you're absorbing stories. Every movement invites explanation: "Why did this go down?" "What if that trend continues?" "Should I act before it's too late?" These micro-narratives create emotional urgency where none is warranted.

The most successful investors in history—from Warren Buffett to John Bogle—have emphasised the importance of detachment. Not because they didn't care, but because they understood that overinvolvement introduces noise and diminishes discipline. Buffett famously said, "The stock market is designed to transfer money from the active to the patient." That transfer begins the moment one starts checking instead of trusting.

This is where the concept of the *blindfold technique* becomes powerful—not as recklessness, but as *designated inattention.* The idea is to create a structured system so reliable, so well-aligned with your goals and values, that it can be left alone for extended periods without compromising its effectiveness. The blindfold is not about ignorance. It's about intentional disengagement. It's about saying, "I have designed this well enough that I do not need to watch it every day."

In practice, this might mean establishing a rule: no portfolio checks more than once per quarter. Or better, designate a specific "review day" twice a year, during which you evaluate performance, rebalance if needed, and review your goals. Outside of those windows, the system runs untouched. This deliberate rhythm not only restores emotional clarity—it also reduces the friction of decision fatigue. You reclaim cognitive space previously occupied by noise.

For most investors, the greatest risk is not market collapse. It is behavioural inconsistency. It is the series of small, seemingly reasonable tweaks made under the illusion of "staying informed" that collectively destroy long-term performance. Constant checking acts as an accelerant to this destruction. It shifts your role from strategic designer to reactive participant—from architect to micromanager. And micromanagement is the antithesis of compounding.

There's an instructive example from the investment committee of a major university endowment. During internal audits, it was discovered that the highest-performing subset of their legacy accounts were those that had been forgotten—accounts where the original donor had passed away, and no one had touched the allocation in decades. These portfolios, left entirely to time and market forces, outperformed most of the actively managed ones. The irony is almost poetic: the best performance came from *complete disengagement.* Not because inaction is always superior, but because intervention is usually mistimed.

Psychologists studying the neuroscience of decision-making have shown that *the urge to check*—whether it's a stock app, social media, or a messaging platform—activates the same dopamine loops as gambling. Each check is a bid for reward, for feedback, for reassurance. But investing is not a slot machine. It is a slow, compounding mechanism that thrives on boredom and indifference. The need to feel something is precisely what undermines the results.

The modern financial landscape, however, makes restraint difficult. Portfolio dashboards are beautifully designed, intuitive, and gamified. Real-time updates, alerts, colour-coded trends—all of it is built to keep you coming back. But the investor must recognise: the platform's incentives are not aligned with yours. What benefits the product (engagement) harms the user (reactivity). Stepping away is not neglect. It is mastery.

One might argue: "But shouldn't I be informed?" The answer is yes—but *periodically, not perpetually*. Being informed means understanding your strategy, your risk exposure, your objectives, and your plan for review. It does not mean watching the market oscillate every hour. If your system is fragile enough to require constant observation, it isn't a system. It's a source of anxiety with a balance sheet.

The cost of checking is not just cognitive. It is emotional erosion. It is the slow degradation of your conviction, your patience, and your trust in the process. It's a quiet bleed—not of capital, but of confidence. And confidence is the compounding agent behind every great investing outcome.

Learning to "check less" is not passive. It is a deliberate discipline. It requires a shift from performance-based validation to purpose-based clarity. You build a system, you design for volatility, you establish rules—and then you *trust it.* The blindfold technique isn't about blindness. It's about choosing where to place your gaze. You focus on the architecture, not the noise. You invest your attention in the plan, not the panic.

In the end, a well-built financial life should offer space, not demand scrutiny. The measure of its quality is not how often it is watched, but how rarely it requires watching. The best investment system is the one that disappears into the background of a life well-lived. The next time you feel the itch to check, pause and ask: *Am I seeking insight—or reassurance?* And if it's the latter, remember—reassurance is not found in data. It is built through design.

Feel Rich, Think Lazy

Wealth, in its truest form, is not a number—it's a state of mind. Yet most investors have been conditioned to pursue performance metrics that often sabotage their well-being. Portfolios may rise, but peace does not necessarily follow. For many, the financial world is not a means to freedom, but a theatre of tension—benchmarks, comparisons, rebalancing alerts, and an endless parade of "what-if" scenarios. In this climate, even the affluent are anxious. The millionaire checks their balance daily. The retiree feels more uncertain now than when they were accumulating. The high earner wonders why abundance still feels precarious. What is missing isn't money. It's *mental architecture.*

To feel rich, you must think differently. You must rewire your internal relationship with time, risk, and reward—not by trying harder, but by stepping back. The lazy investor is not inattentive. They are *deliberate.* Their genius lies in detachment, not denial. The phrase "feel rich, think lazy" is a philosophical reset, a reminder that financial serenity is built not from squeezing performance out of every investment, but from designing a system that serves your life—not consumes it.

The problem begins with a performance-first mindset. Modern finance worships metrics—alpha, Sharpe ratios, drawdowns, CAGR. While these tools have technical merit, they are often internalised as emotional benchmarks. The result is a kind of inner scoreboard that's always running. Did I beat the market this quarter? Am I on track for retirement at 58 instead of 60? Could I have made more if I'd allocated more to tech? These questions, repeated daily, become a script of insufficiency. It doesn't matter that the portfolio is growing. The experience is one of lack, not gain. This mindset is self-defeating. The more you chase optimisation, the more fragile your satisfaction becomes.

Consider two investors with identical portfolios. One reviews their account monthly, the other annually. Statistically, their outcomes may be nearly identical over time, but their experiences of those outcomes will diverge dramatically. The frequent checker will ride emotional rollercoasters—volatility interpreted as threat, underperformance interpreted as failure. The infrequent checker? More likely to see a stable upward trend, precisely because their lens filters out noise. This is not about naivety. It is about protecting *cognitive margin.*

The true goal of investing is not to outperform others—it is to *not need to think about money all the time.* The ability to go through your day without checking your balance, reading headlines, or second-guessing your future is a form of wealth in itself. But achieving that state requires a kind of emotional reconditioning that runs counter to modern cultural incentives. The world says: pay attention, hustle harder, react fast. The wise investor learns to say: automate, detach, trust the design.

Reframing wealth means asking better questions. Not "How can I earn more?" but "What do I want money to protect?" Not "How can I squeeze 1% more return?" but "What risks am I willing to ignore?" These are not theoretical musings—they are the backbone of durable financial confidence. By thinking like a lazy investor, you begin to structure your finances around your *values*, not your fears. You stop optimising for headlines and start designing for habits.

One of the most effective ways to build this mindset is to invert the typical approach to investing. Rather than starting with assets, start with your *calendar*. Ask: "What do I want my weeks and years to feel like?" From there, reverse-engineer the simplest portfolio structure that supports that lifestyle without ongoing input. If the system you design requires constant checking or emotional calibration, it's not finished. Think of it like an irrigation system: once installed, it should water your garden whether or not you're paying attention.

This is not laziness in the colloquial sense. It is *strategic conservation*. Your time and attention are finite resources. Wasting them on market speculation or emotional turbulence is a poor allocation of your scarcest capital. Thinking lazy means you preserve your attention for things that compound in value—your health, your relationships, your creativity—not minute-by-minute market moves.

Importantly, the framework of thinking lazy does not imply indifference to outcomes. It implies mastery over inputs. You define the parameters of your portfolio—risk tolerance, allocation, time horizon—up front. You build guardrails. You automate contributions. Then you step back, not out of neglect, but out of respect for the system you've designed. Emotional detachment is not a sign of disengagement. It's the clearest indicator that you trust the process.

Contrast this with the hyper-attuned investor. Despite high intelligence and technical skill, they live in a constant loop of stimulus and response. Every new market event reopens the question of whether they're doing the right thing. Their portfolios are sculpted to precision, but their peace of mind is in pieces. This is not an information problem. It's an *identity problem*. They are measuring success by proximity to perfection, instead of alignment with peace.

To move beyond this trap, it helps to think in terms of identity. Are you the type of person who is constantly adjusting, reacting, comparing—or the type who is quietly confident in the long-term design? The distinction is not trivial. It shapes the architecture of your entire financial life. Identity-driven investors don't rely on willpower to stay the course. They rely on *systems that reflect who they already believe themselves to be.*

This is why financial minimalism is not about simplicity for simplicity's sake. It's about removing the psychological clutter that clouds decision-making. If you can achieve your goals with a three-fund portfolio and a biannual review, why opt for something more complicated? Because it feels sophisticated? Because it keeps you busy? These are emotional justifications masquerading as strategy. They serve the ego, not the outcome.

Reconditioning your emotions around money also involves re-examining your media diet. The financial media ecosystem thrives on urgency and novelty. Its business model is attention, not accuracy. To think like a lazy investor is to exit that ecosystem—either by consuming less, or by filtering ruthlessly. Read less frequently, but with more depth. Replace scrolling with reflection. Trust data over drama.

There's also the matter of language. Many investors unknowingly reinforce unhealthy patterns through the words they use: "I need to win," "I hope this works," "I should have known." These phrases introduce judgement where there should be structure. A more constructive vocabulary is grounded in design: "This is my framework," "I've accounted for volatility," "My rules are in place." Language shapes emotion. Emotion shapes behaviour. Behaviour shapes outcome.

Feeling rich has almost nothing to do with the size of your balance sheet. It is a product of *psychological slack*—the margin between your financial system and your emotional demands. When your system requires constant oversight or delivers constant doubt, no amount of money can make you feel wealthy. But when your system is aligned, automated, and resilient to your own instincts, wealth becomes quiet. It becomes background music to a well-scored life.

The final shift is perhaps the most profound: you begin to decouple *external returns* from *internal rewards*. A good investment year is not one in which you beat the market. It's one in which you followed your principles. It's one in which you felt free to focus elsewhere—on your family, your health, your purpose—because your money was working quietly and competently in the background.

To feel rich is to feel stable, unhurried, and undisturbed. To think lazy is to have earned that serenity through intelligent, intentional design. This is the art of the truly wealthy—not those who have the most, but those who need to *do* the least to sustain what matters most.

Chapter 4
The Serenity Portfolio

If financial markets rewarded sheer intellect alone, the wealthiest individuals would always be the most informed. Yet, repeatedly, the evidence tells a different story. Long-term investing success hinges less on constant access to information than on the careful design of systems and emotional discipline. The Serenity Portfolio rests on a striking premise: the most effective portfolio is not the one that makes you feel clever, but the one you can almost forget you own.

Reaching this state of calm disengagement requires more than mere apathy. It demands intentional architecture—structures that anticipate human error, absorb volatility, and operate independently of your daily attention. This chapter examines how to construct an investment system that not only endures your absence but thrives on it. The Serenity Portfolio is more than metaphor; it is method: a framework informed by behavioural insight, probabilistic reasoning, and structural elegance.

Most investors falter not from ignorance but from overinvolvement. A constant urge to monitor, tweak, and optimise often produces worse outcomes—both financially and psychologically. When a portfolio commands your attention, it ceases to be a tool of liberation; it becomes a source of strain. Society conditions us to equate busyness with prudence, presence with responsibility. But what if the apex of financial maturity lies in confident non-intervention?

Designing for disengagement begins with an uncomfortable recognition: the primary source of friction in your portfolio is not inflation, taxes, or fees—it is you. Your impulses, your well-intentioned adjustments, your compulsive rebalancing. The Serenity Portfolio neutralises this vulnerability at its root. It encourages the creation of systems so robust that they function seamlessly while you focus elsewhere—whether travelling, raising children, or simply choosing to live. This is not laziness; it is resilience deliberately engineered.

A common misconception in passive investing is equating low effort with low principle. In truth, lazy investing—properly executed—is structured, disciplined minimalism. The Serenity Portfolio is underpinned by rigorous upfront work: a coherent allocation strategy, calibrated risk exposure, behavioural safeguards, and operational simplicity. It is not "set and forget"; it is "set so well you can afford to forget." That subtle distinction is pivotal.

The most successful investors do not labour longer; they interfere less. But restraint is rarely innate—it is designed. Picture a thermostat regulating temperature automatically or a kayak that rights itself in turbulent waters. The Serenity Portfolio follows the same philosophy: anticipate disruption, absorb volatility, and let structure manage the inevitable. Crises will occur. Markets will fluctuate. A portfolio built with antifragility not only survives these stresses—it may benefit from them.

Antifragility, a term popularised by Nassim Taleb, deserves careful attention. Robustness merely survives stress; antifragility improves because of it. A well-crafted Serenity Portfolio does not simply weather market swings; it harnesses them to accelerate compounding. This often involves favouring equities over bonds, value over growth, or global diversification, always designing for the inevitable, never for the ideal scenario.

None of this matters if the portfolio fails the sleep test. Can you rest without checking balances? A week, a month, a quarter? If the answer is no, your portfolio may be technically sound but emotionally compromised. The Serenity Portfolio explicitly optimises for peace of mind as much as returns, prioritising sustainable calm per unit of risk over maximal theoretical gain.

Consider a practical example: a 38-year-old professional with a moderate-high income builds a diversified portfolio—60% global equities, 30% short-term government bonds, 10% REITs—automating monthly contributions and rebalancing annually, while avoiding financial news entirely. Over twenty years, she may underperform a hyperactive trader by a fraction of a percent annually. Yet she experiences none of the stress, sidesteps behavioural pitfalls, and accumulates comparable wealth. More importantly, she spends those years living her life, not micromanaging it.

Empirical studies reinforce this approach. Analyses from Vanguard, Morningstar, and DALBAR consistently show that average investors underperform their own investments—not due to poor instruments, but due to emotional mismanagement. The Serenity Portfolio interrupts this self-sabotage, acting as a buffer against both market volatility and human error.

Adopting a Serenity mindset reframes what it means to be a competent investor. Success is no longer measured by predictive prowess, timing, or real-time insight. It is measured by the discipline to honour a system designed intelligently from the outset. In essence, you are not the pilot navigating turbulence; you are the engineer who calibrated the autopilot. And if that autopilot is sound, your primary responsibility is restraint.

This does not remove responsibility—it concentrates it. Constructing a Serenity Portfolio requires intellectual rigour: careful goal-setting, risk calibration, and pre-emptive decisions that will later be tested emotionally. The payoff is autonomy: a portfolio immune to mood swings, schedule disruptions, or fleeting opinions. Responsibility is front-loaded, yielding freedom in the future.

This chapter will explore how to achieve this: strategies that prioritise longevity over reactivity, frameworks for assessing true autonomy, and principles that translate antifragility into actionable design. Portfolios will be examined not only through performance metrics but through their ability to endure stress—job loss, market collapse, inflation, and personal upheaval. The "lazy" investor, armed with systemic sophistication, often outperforms the frenetic counterpart both financially and psychologically.

The Serenity Portfolio is not avoidance—it is mastery through absence. When your money thrives independently, your mind is liberated to engage more fully with life. The objective transcends financial independence; it is psychological sovereignty: a recognition that your future is secure and that you can afford to think of it less.

This is not complacency—it is the pinnacle of confidence. Here, the lazy investor begins to resemble the truly wise one.

Design for Disengagement

The average investor does not fail for lack of intelligence, resources, or tools. They fail because their system depends on them being present. Emotionally present. Mentally engaged. Constantly informed. That level of demand is not only unrealistic—it's unsustainable. *Design for disengagement* challenges the assumption that good investing requires constant vigilance. Instead, it asks a more elegant question: *What would your investment strategy look like if you weren't allowed to touch it for ten years?* If that thought terrifies you, then your current design is likely built on behavioural fragility, not structural integrity.

The idea that a portfolio should perform best when left alone is not just counterintuitive—it's quietly radical. For decades, mainstream financial culture has romanticised the archetype of the hands-on investor: watchful, data-driven, always adjusting, perpetually alert. But this image is not only exhausting—it's empirically unwise. Every behavioural finance study of the past 30 years tells the same story: hyper-engagement is inversely correlated with long-term returns. Those who intervene least often, and with the clearest predefined rules, tend to outperform those constantly reacting to new information. So, why do we still build systems that need us?

True financial freedom is not about accumulating more capital—it's about needing less management. To that end, we must prioritise *system design over human discipline.* A disengaged portfolio is not a neglected one; it is one that has been deliberately constructed to remove dependency on the investor's attention, moods, or availability. It is a system robust to your distraction, your travel schedule, your family emergencies, or even your complete disinterest. The irony is sharp: the more you build a portfolio that doesn't need you, the more likely it is to serve you faithfully.

Let us consider what this requires. First, disengagement does not absolve the investor of responsibility. Quite the opposite. It front-loads the responsibility into design decisions. Asset allocation must be durable. Risk must be contextually defined. Liquidity needs must be anticipated in advance. This is not laziness masquerading as minimalism. It's strategic automation born of self-awareness. You are not building a castle that requires constant repair; you are laying down stone that weathers the seasons on its own.

One of the most misunderstood aspects of investing is the role of attention. Most people assume that attentiveness equals care, and that care improves outcomes. But in markets, attention often breeds overreaction. When investors check their portfolios daily, they interpret randomness as trend. They interpret volatility as signal. They interpret discomfort as danger. And then they act—rebalancing too frequently, selling too early, hedging unnecessarily. The cost isn't just financial. It's emotional. Constant engagement frays the nerves, distorts judgement, and steals time that could be spent on pursuits of real value.

So how do we design for disengagement in practical terms? We start with allocations that are self-stabilising. This typically includes broad, global index exposure across asset classes that are inherently uncorrelated or differently cyclical. It means avoiding complexity for its own sake. Simplicity is not naivety—it is an acknowledgment of long-term resilience. A portfolio of three or four well-selected, low cost ETFs with global exposure can do more for long-term wealth than a dozen actively managed funds selected with excruciating care. Why? Because the simple portfolio doesn't ask you to second-guess it. It doesn't bait you into tinkering.

Consider the glidepath model used in target-date retirement funds. These funds automatically adjust the risk profile as the investor ages, without any required intervention. Millions of investors who never think about their asset mix again after enrolment end up with portfolios that are safer, better diversified, and more tax-efficient than those managed by amateur enthusiasts. This is not just a win for convenience. It's a demonstration of *behaviourally informed design.* The system works because it does not rely on the user doing anything.

Disengaged systems are not only effective—they are ethical. They respect the cognitive limits of the investor. We all have finite bandwidth. Life does not pause to let us rebalance. Markets do not consult our emotional state before crashing. A portfolio that requires your constant mental presence is, at best, an expensive form of self-delusion. At worst, it is a source of chronic anxiety disguised as financial prudence. To build systems that function *without you* is to build systems that *honour your future self*—the version of you that will inevitably be busy, distracted, or simply uninterested in market minutiae.

A key design principle of disengaged investing is automation. This extends beyond asset allocation to include automated contributions, dividend reinvestment, tax-loss harvesting (where applicable), and even periodic rebalancing. Each of these components, when automated, removes one more decision point. And every decision point removed is one less opportunity for emotion to interfere with logic. It is the difference between a plan that asks for your input and one that protects you from it.

The philosophy of disengagement also draws strength from the concept of redundancy. A well-designed system should include buffers—emergency cash reserves, staggered maturity dates, low debt exposure—so that a temporary crisis in your personal life does not require you to tamper with your investments. Redundancy, in this context, is not wasteful. It is wise. It ensures that the portfolio is not a brittle machine that breaks under pressure, but a living system that adapts and absorbs.

There is an important shift in identity that accompanies this approach. You are no longer the *operator* of your investment strategy. You are the *architect.* Operators respond to noise, to stimuli, to changes. Architects step back. They plan once—carefully—and then allow the structure to hold. That doesn't mean there is never review or revision. It means that such moments are rare, intentional, and governed by rules—not by mood or headlines. Designing for disengagement is about engineering *out* the operator impulse.

To illustrate this further, consider the contrast between two investors: one checks the markets daily, reads five financial newsletters, and frequently rotates between asset classes based on perceived opportunities. The other sets up a globally diversified portfolio, contributes monthly, and checks in once a year for a scheduled rebalance. Over a 20-year span, the second investor almost always ends up wealthier—not because they were smarter, but because their system was more *forgiving of their humanity*. The first investor, by contrast, mistook attention for mastery—and paid the price.

Ultimately, to design for disengagement is to acknowledge that the best systems are those that succeed *despite* our imperfections. You are not designing for the idealised, disciplined, rational version of yourself. You are designing for the real, distracted, emotionally inconsistent human being you actually are. And that is not an admission of weakness. It is a profound expression of self-knowledge.

The Serenity Portfolio, as a concept, depends entirely on this principle. It is not a prescription for apathy—it is a blueprint for autonomy. You must still care enough to care once. But if you do that work thoroughly, you earn the right to step back without penalty. That is the dividend of disengagement: a life that is financially coherent without being financially consumed.

And this is the paradox at the heart of wise investing: *The less your system needs you, the more it gives you.* Not just in wealth, but in time, calm, and clarity. When the design is sound, you can afford to look away. And when you can look away, you can finally look at everything else that matters.

Lazy Is Not Reckless

There is a persistent and costly misunderstanding in the world of personal finance: that effort equals merit, and that reduced effort must reflect reduced seriousness. Nowhere is this more misleading than in investing. *Lazy investing*, as advocated in this book, is not the abdication of responsibility. It is the concentrated expression of it. To operate with minimal ongoing input, a system must be designed with exceptional care. The paradox is this: the lazy investor is not the one who avoids work, but the one who front-loads it so intelligently that most future work becomes unnecessary.

To dismiss laziness in this context as a vice is to mistake motion for mastery. Busyness, tinkering, the endless search for optimisation—these are not badges of diligence. More often, they are signs of poorly conceived systems. The market does not reward the investor who tries harder. It rewards the investor who *interferes less*. But to earn the right to do less, one must do the hard thinking upfront: defining principles, setting constraints, and aligning methods with long-term outcomes.

This chapter's core assertion is simple: *lazy does not mean reckless*. It means rigorous design, executed with enough clarity and discipline that the system continues to function even in your absence. A reckless investor builds a system that demands their constant input. A lazy investor builds one that thrives without them. The difference is not just one of temperament—it is one of architecture.

Consider the analogy of a pilot versus an engineer. A reckless investor wants to fly the plane constantly, hands on every control, reacting to every bump in the air. The lazy investor is more like the aerospace engineer: they build autopilot systems that manage turbulence, altitude, and trajectory without constant human override. Both care about reaching the destination. One trusts a machine of their own design. The other never sleeps.

To build an investment system worthy of disengagement, the lazy investor must take five steps upfront—each of which demands focus, clarity, and an unsentimental relationship with risk.

First: define what wealth means *to you.* This is not a slogan. It's a requirement. Without a personal definition of enough, the investor is a slave to moving targets—net worth goals that shift every time someone else's number appears on a screen. Reckless investors conflate wealth with status. Lazy investors anchor it to autonomy. If you cannot articulate what a successful investment outcome looks like in concrete, non-performance-based terms, you will never stop chasing—and tweaking.

Second: adopt a default allocation. This is your anchor. It should reflect your true risk tolerance, not your aspirational one. A lazy portfolio is not aggressive or conservative—it is *honest.* A globally diversified mix of low-cost index funds may seem unexciting, but it is resilient. Its strength lies in what it does not require: no market timing, no forecasting, no sector bets. Once designed, it serves as a base case that does not need defending every time the headlines shift.

Third: install behavioural guardrails. This includes automated contributions, scheduled rebalancing (once or twice a year, maximum), and *a policy for when you are allowed to review or adjust the portfolio.* If the answer is "whenever I feel nervous," the system is already compromised. Lazy investors pre-commit. They establish protocols *before* volatility tests their resolve. Reckless investors rely on memory and mood, believing they'll make good decisions when it matters most. History suggests otherwise.

Fourth: design for neglect. A lazy portfolio must be robust to periods of distraction, apathy, illness, or even complete withdrawal. If your investment system cannot survive six months of inattention, it was never robust to begin with. Many high-net-worth individuals quietly admit to stepping away from their portfolios for years—sometimes out of disinterest, sometimes due to life circumstances. The ones who thrive financially are those whose systems didn't penalise them for doing so. The structure protected them from themselves.

Fifth: write an investor's constitution. This may sound ceremonial, but it is critical. Your constitution should outline your investment principles, your chosen strategy, your behavioural limits, and your reasons. It exists not for legal protection, but as a psychological anchor. When fear tempts you to change your plan, you read what your past self—clear-headed, detached, and rational—wrote about what matters. That act alone can prevent thousands in opportunity cost and years of recovery.

This upfront labour is not optional. It is the price of freedom. Lazy investing does not bypass effort—it *compresses* it into moments that matter. The work is not constant, but it is concentrated. Lazy investors do not avoid discipline; they bake it into the system.

The broader cultural misunderstanding of laziness is a barrier here. In Western work culture especially, there is an unspoken worship of exertion. Effort is assumed to be noble. Stillness, suspect. This thinking is disastrous in the context of investing. A system that requires your constant attention is not a sign of excellence—it is a failure of planning. True mastery is building systems that *work without you.* Lazy investors respect their future selves too much to make them carry the burden indefinitely.

Let's examine a practical example: two investors start with £500,000. One builds a portfolio of global index funds, automates contributions, sets a once-a-year review date, and documents their rules for selling. The other assembles a hand-picked portfolio of 22 stocks across tech, healthcare, and energy, monitors Bloomberg daily, subscribes to three market newsletters, and adjusts positions weekly. Ten years later, it is not just that the first investor has likely outperformed—statistically, that's probable. More importantly, they've spent less than five hours a year on their portfolio. The second has spent five hours a week. One has peace. The other has a spreadsheet full of regrets.

This is not a call to disengage blindly. It is a call to structure your system so that disengagement is safe. Recklessness is abandoning principles. Laziness, when applied with rigour, *requires* them. The lazy investor is accountable to a higher standard: one that forces them to clarify what they believe before the market tests it. This is why laziness—done correctly—is hard to fake. It cannot be improvised. It must be earned.

The language we use matters. When someone says, "I don't want to think about my investments all the time," they are often treated as unserious. But what if that's the most serious investor in the room? What if they've spent years designing a system they trust so deeply that it requires no further energy? This is not negligence. It is maturity. It is a refusal to allow wealth to dominate the psyche.

Lazy investing, then, is not for everyone. It is not for those addicted to activity, performance-chasing, or the emotional highs of winning bets. It is for those who want *more than just returns.* They want reliability. Simplicity. Autonomy. Peace. That outcome is not achieved by ignoring your investments—it is achieved by designing them so that ignoring them is *rational.*

Every system is a contract between your present and future self. Lazy investors negotiate well. They front-load effort so that future versions of themselves can focus on what matters more than money. This is not just a technical shift. It is a philosophical one. A reorientation away from performance, status, and excitement—toward consistency, clarity, and calm.

There is no shame in laziness when it is principled, purposeful, and premeditated. If anything, it is the mark of someone who understands that their time—and peace of mind—is more valuable than one more attempt to "beat the market." They are not underachieving. They are strategically absent. And that absence, far from reckless, is often what delivers the richest results.

The Antifragile Allocation

Most portfolios are designed to survive. Few are designed to benefit from disorder. This is a subtle yet defining distinction—one that separates systems built for fragility from those wired for resilience, and resilience from something rarer still: *antifragility*. Coined and elaborated by Nassim Nicholas Taleb, antifragility refers to systems that improve under stress, volatility, and chaos. They don't merely endure shocks—they feed on them. For the lazy investor, this concept holds profound value. It suggests the possibility of a portfolio that, once properly constructed, does not just tolerate your absence and the market's wildness—but is *enhanced* by both.

In traditional thinking, risk is framed almost exclusively as threat. Volatility, noise, disorder—these are seen as dangers to be managed, avoided, hedged against. But antifragility inverts this framing. It reframes volatility as a source of optionality, asymmetry, and growth. The question is not, "How can I make my portfolio safe?" but rather, "How can I design a system that *gains* from shocks, unpredictability, and even neglect?" This question, properly asked, shifts the investor from a defensive mindset into a design-driven one. The antifragile investor is not risk-averse—they are *fragility-averse.* And that distinction opens the door to both philosophical clarity and practical innovation.

The antifragile allocation begins with a foundational insight: *exposure to upsides should be uncapped; exposure to downsides, strictly limited.* This is not achieved by guessing which asset will go up. It is achieved by deliberately constructing a barbell-shaped portfolio—a configuration Taleb has advocated—where the vast majority of capital is placed in ultra-safe assets, while a small, capped portion is reserved for high-risk, high-upside bets. The genius is not in predicting which moonshot will work. It's in knowing that only one needs to. The safety net is vast. The speculative portion is optionality-rich. And crucially, this structure does not require constant input or precise foresight.

Let's ground this in real terms. Imagine an investor who allocates 85% of their capital to short-term government bonds or cash equivalents—assets unlikely to be wiped out, even in a crisis. The remaining 15% is invested in asymmetric opportunities: venture capital funds, deep-value stocks, distressed assets, or highly volatile but convex instruments like long-dated call options on innovation-focused ETFs. The lazy investor does not watch these instruments daily. They understand that 9 out of 10 might go nowhere. But the one that succeeds can more than compensate—and because the base of the portfolio is conservative, drawdowns are manageable and recoverable.

Antifragile portfolios benefit from *nonlinearity*. A fragile asset has a downside greater than its upside. A robust asset has a symmetrical risk-reward trade-off. But an antifragile one has limited losses and uncapped gains. This structure naturally aligns with a lazy investment philosophy: *it favours non-intervention.* You do not need to guess short-term price movements. You need only ensure that the structure allows serendipity and randomness to do their work, uninterrupted.

Importantly, antifragile investing is not the same as high-risk investing. Reckless investors place large bets on uncertain outcomes. Antifragile investors place *small* bets on those same outcomes—intentionally designed so that loss is survivable but gain is transformational. The allocation is the secret. The position sizing is the power. What looks like passivity is in fact engineering. Volatility is not feared—it is invited, because the system feeds off it.

This principle can be extended to public markets. Consider the investor who blends an 80% allocation to low-volatility, dividend-paying global index funds with a 20% allocation to early-stage technology ETFs or frontier-market exposure. The former provides ballast; the latter introduces exposure to convexity. No active monitoring required. Just periodic rebalancing. The portfolio is not immune to drawdowns, but the drawdowns are not existential. They're the cost of maintaining optionality. Over time, as some of the asymmetric assets compound dramatically—or fail quietly—the investor reaps the payoff not of insight, but of structure.

There is also an emotional dimension. Antifragile portfolios are psychologically protective. They relieve the investor from the impossible burden of predicting the future. Instead of constantly scanning for threats, they adopt a posture of receptivity. The design absorbs shocks. It doesn't demand vigilance. This enables the investor to cultivate the rarest and most underrated trait in finance: detachment. A lazy investor cannot afford a system that panics when they're not looking. They need one that *improves* when they're not looking. That is the promise of antifragility.

But it must be earned. A true antifragile portfolio requires more than diversification. It requires deliberate asymmetry, intelligent capital partitioning, and the restraint to leave it alone. Taleb writes that the antifragile system requires *"less understanding, more convexity."* That is to say, your edge is not in forecasting, but in designing systems that don't punish you for being wrong—and reward you massively when right. For the lazy investor, this principle is liberating. You don't need to be a market genius. You just need to avoid fragility and let probability work in your favour.

Consider the counterexample. Most conventional portfolios are overfitted to yesterday's calm. They assume linearity, continuity, and mean-reversion. When a real shock arrives—2008, 2020, or the next unnameable event—they break down precisely because they were built for the wrong world. They need supervision, explanation, management. The antifragile portfolio does not. It anticipates disorder. It embeds disorder. It makes peace with disorder. And in doing so, it sidesteps the two forces that destroy most investors: the compulsion to react, and the assumption of control.

There's also a deeper insight here, one that touches the philosophical core of this book: *not all returns are financial.* The serenity of owning a portfolio that gets stronger under pressure is a psychological asset of immense value. Knowing you do not have to check the markets daily because your structure has already accounted for the unknown—is worth more than a few basis points of alpha. It is a freedom that compounds. Not on a spreadsheet, but in your daily experience of time, energy, and autonomy.

To be clear, antifragile allocations are not infallible. They require thought, testing, and periodic recalibration. But once set, they reward patience—not tinkering. They reward volatility—not prediction. And they reward presence—not constant presence, but the capacity to be present *where your time actually matters*. That is the quiet power at the heart of antifragility. It is not loud, flashy, or widely advertised. But it is deeply aligned with the lazy investor's most valuable outcome: long-term peace through short-term tolerance of chaos.

The antifragile investor does not try to outwit the market. They try to outlive it. They understand that neglect, when combined with the right structure, is not negligence. It is strategy. They do not eliminate risk. They harness it. They build portfolios that do not merely hold during volatility—but learn from it. That is not luck. That is design. And it is precisely the kind of design that frees the investor—not just from fragility, but from the exhausting, endless effort to manage what was never manageable to begin with.

Sleep-Tested Strategies

The ultimate test of an investment plan is not its performance on a spreadsheet, but its effect on your sleep. If your portfolio is statistically sound but emotionally disruptive—if it demands constant attention, sparks chronic doubt, or robs your mind of stillness—it is, by definition, poorly designed. The most effective investment strategies are not those that maximise returns at any cost, but those that *minimise regret, resist overreaction, and allow the investor to disengage without distress*. In other words, they are *sleep-tested*—engineered not for applause, but for peace.

The standard language of finance is riddled with benchmarks, volatility metrics, Sharpe ratios, and annualised returns. But rarely does it ask: *How does this strategy feel in the middle of the night, when markets are down, and news feeds are screaming?* That question, though rarely quantified, is central to durable wealth creation. It determines whether an investor sticks with the plan during turbulence—or abandons it precisely when perseverance is most needed. The ability to sleep at night is not a trivial side effect. It is a core feature of any successful long-term strategy.

This concept does not imply softness or timidity. It does not suggest avoiding risk altogether. Rather, it argues for *alignment*—between one's portfolio design and one's psychological constitution. A sleep-tested strategy is one that anticipates your emotional limits and bakes them into the architecture of your investments. It knows that you are not a robot. It respects the realities of stress, distraction, and attention fatigue. It protects you not only from market losses, but from *your own worst impulses*.

Take, for example, the classic 60/40 portfolio—60% equities, 40% bonds. For decades, it has served as a reliable foundation for investors seeking balanced exposure to growth and stability. While critics have argued that it is outdated in a low-yield, high-volatility world, the deeper truth is that the 60/40 framework remains compelling not because it is mathematically optimal in every scenario, but because it is *emotionally absorbable*. It offers ballast during sell-offs, cushions against behavioural panic, and requires minimal daily oversight. It may not maximise returns in every year, but it maximises *endurance*. And endurance is what builds wealth.

Contrast this with a more aggressive strategy—say, a 90% equity portfolio focused on emerging markets, tech startups, or high-beta growth names. On paper, the upside potential is immense. But when volatility hits—and it will—the investor must not only endure drawdowns, but also withstand the psychological dissonance that comes from watching their net worth fluctuate wildly. Very few people can do this consistently without breaking discipline. The point is not that aggressive portfolios are wrong, but that *their cost is rarely just financial.* The mental bandwidth they consume often exceeds their performance benefit.

This is where the lazy investor's philosophy becomes a hidden advantage. By *intentionally deprioritising daily optimisation*, the lazy investor is forced to construct a system that can run itself. That constraint leads, almost inevitably, to simpler, sturdier, and more emotionally sustainable plans. It produces portfolios that prioritise *structure over speculation, clarity over cleverness, and rest over reaction.* These portfolios may not beat the market every year—but they often outperform where it matters most: in adherence, longevity, and internal coherence.

Consider an investor who builds their core portfolio around three low-cost index funds: one global equity tracker, one domestic bond fund, and one inflation-linked asset (such as TIPS or gold). They allocate according to their personal risk profile—say 50/30/20—and rebalance once a year, or not at all unless allocations drift substantially. They check their portfolio quarterly at most. They do not track financial news. They do not attempt tactical tilts based on macro forecasts. They accept volatility as a feature, not a bug. The result? They may not achieve "perfect" returns. But they preserve mental clarity, reduce trading errors, and free up enormous cognitive space.

This design reflects what Daniel Kahneman called *experienced utility*—the lived emotional quality of an activity—not just its calculated utility. Most investors dramatically underestimate the emotional toll of constant exposure to markets. The daily watching, the refreshing, the comparison to others, the what-if thinking—all of it creates noise that contaminates decision-making. A portfolio that removes this noise not only improves emotional health, but also increases the odds of remaining invested during downturns—when compounding actually matters most.

Moreover, sleep-tested strategies embed a concept of *intentional limits.* These are not constraints of performance, but of interference. The lazy investor is not trying to fine-tune their way to superiority. They are trying to *eliminate the conditions that cause investors to sabotage themselves.* That includes overly complex asset allocations, excessive leverage, unclear exit rules, and dependence on market timing. Simplicity, transparency, and procedural clarity become the pillars of design.

One illustrative approach is the "Boglehead" model—a philosophy inspired by Vanguard founder Jack Bogle, which favours extreme simplicity and relentless cost discipline. It usually involves holding two or three total-market index funds, rebalancing infrequently, and ignoring media noise entirely. Its results have been staggering—not necessarily because of superior asset selection, but because *the behavioural drag is near zero.* Investors using this model typically trade less, panic less, and stay invested longer. That's the real edge.

Another example comes from the permanent portfolio approach championed by Harry Browne: 25% stocks, 25% long-term bonds, 25% cash, 25% gold. It's not a strategy designed to "win" in any one environment—but to survive *every* environment. While its long-term returns may lag the S&P 500, its emotional volatility is substantially lower. The investor who sleeps through 2008 and 2020—who neither sells at the bottom nor chases fads at the top—often ends up with better outcomes *precisely because they were not trying to outperform in the first place.*

Critically, this chapter is not an argument against performance. It is an argument against *fragile performance*—the kind that looks brilliant on paper but collapses in the real world because the human behind the plan cannot stick with it. An elegant model that fails under emotional pressure is worse than a dull one that endures. The defining feature of sleep-tested strategies is not intellectual complexity, but *psychological realism.* They start from the assumption that attention is a finite resource, stress is cumulative, and the investor's greatest risk is not the market—but themselves.

This reframing leads us to the idea of *emotional returns*—the psychological benefits derived from holding a portfolio that doesn't nag at your mind. That doesn't require you to constantly second-guess yourself. That doesn't make you feel inadequate or anxious when other investors are boasting of higher returns. Emotional returns are not separate from financial returns—they are *enablers* of financial returns. Because they increase the odds that you will stay consistent, keep contributing, and resist impulsive mistakes.

Sleep-tested strategies also align with a broader life philosophy: that money is not the goal, but the enabler. If your portfolio consumes more time than it frees, something has gone wrong. The ideal investment system is one you can *forget about most of the time.* That does not mean irresponsibility. It means maturity. It means designing with foresight, so that day-to-day fluctuations become irrelevant background noise rather than front-page stressors. It means building a plan that respects not just your financial targets, but your *psychological dignity.*

Ultimately, sleep-tested investing is not a strategy. It is a worldview. It says: I would rather compound slowly with peace than chase aggressively with unrest. I would rather be dull and durable than brilliant and brittle. I would rather build a system that serves my life than a system that *requires* my life to serve it. This is not a compromise. It is clarity. And it is the foundation upon which long-term wealth—not just measured in money, but in time, energy, and calm—can reliably be built.

Chapter 5
Time, the Ultimate Asset

If money is the visible instrument of investing, time is its hidden engine—patient, persistent, and largely invisible. Yet despite endless debate over risk tolerance, allocation, and market timing, time remains the most neglected and misunderstood variable in wealth creation. Investors often treat it as a neutral backdrop, a passive stage upon which strategies perform, when in truth it is the medium that grants those strategies their power. Most people think they are managing money, when they are, in reality, managing their relationship with time.

The lazy investor apprehends this distinction intuitively. Not because they are disengaged, but because they exercise discernment in what they choose to influence. Time is not something to outrun; it is to be aligned with. Real investment success rarely comes from doing more or knowing more—it emerges from surrendering to compounding sooner than most. Portfolios are constructed to sit, not sprint. Decisions are made to endure, not merely to impress. Systems are designed to leverage duration rather than frantic activity.

At the core of this chapter lies a provocative notion: compounding is more than mathematics; it is a philosophy of life. The exponential curve familiar to finance is also a metaphor for restraint, patience, and the humility to allow growth its own rhythm. Deviations from a long-term plan are not mere technical errors—they are interruptions in the most powerful engine of finance. And almost invariably, those interruptions arise not from ignorance, but from impatience.

Modern finance, ironically, idolises speed. News cycles compress. Apps deliver instant quotes. Analysts recalibrate quarterly. Urgency sells products, and so the industry promotes it relentlessly. Yet compounding remains indifferent to pace. It operates at one tempo: gradual at first, then astonishingly rapid. The only path to its reward is patient endurance. The lazy investor's advantage is not idleness, but disciplined stillness—knowing when not to act. They cultivate temporal awareness, not passivity; they are deliberate, not slow.

This reorientation reshapes the traditional calculus of investing. Focus shifts from today's fluctuations to outcomes a decade hence. This principle underpins what we term the Decade Decision Rule: any investment choice must make sense ten years out, not ten days. It is a tool to filter out noise, emotional temptation, and analytical overreach. In essence, it asks: will this decision honour the compounding trajectory, or will it undermine it?

An agricultural analogy helps illuminate this idea. A farmer may overfertilise, replant incessantly, and micromanage crops—or they may cultivate soil quality, trust seasonal cycles, and invest in long-maturing varieties. The second approach produces less drama, yet greater resilience and yield. Investing mirrors this: chasing trades and obsessively rebalancing creates illusionary control, but often at the cost of friction, expense, and behavioural drag. True wealth is usually grown quietly, in portfolios left undisturbed long enough to flourish.

Evidence supports this. Fidelity once noted that the top-performing accounts were often those that had been largely forgotten. Time outperforms attention. The less interference, the more compounding can work its quiet magic. The lazy investor does not merely tolerate time; they exploit it strategically.

This chapter also examines the subtle tension between time and uncertainty. Time magnifies both upside and ambiguity. Outcomes stretch over decades, rewarding patience but testing confidence. Many investors falter not for lack of knowledge, but for lack of emotional endurance. Here, the lazy investor holds an edge: by refusing to respond to every fluctuation, they decouple action from anxiety, trusting the system more than the signal, recognising that what truly matters is sustained performance over time.

Consider the Patience Premium—the notion that markets reward those willing to wait. Longer horizons tend to deliver higher expected returns, not by mysticism, but because impatience is common. Attention spans are short, incentives misaligned, and emotions fragile. The market acts as a behavioural filter, favouring those who can endure. The lazy investor does not outsmart others—they simply avoid disqualifying themselves.

Philosophically, this is emotional aikido: redirecting energy rather than resisting it. Volatility becomes an ally, provided one remains still. Compounding itself exemplifies this principle—it demands no genius, only faith in duration. Yet faith is hard to cultivate in a culture obsessed with immediacy. The lazy investor counters this cultural impulse, reminding us that slowness is not weakness, but carefully placed wisdom.

Throughout the chapter, we explore why time is so difficult to trust, how modern life erodes patience, and what it truly means to build a strategy optimised for the long arc. Lessons from Stoicism, Buddhism, and Christian monasticism reinforce this mindset: small, consistent actions over time transform lives. Real-world examples illustrate how inactivity—executed intelligently—can be a source of advantage. Tools such as the Decade Filter help investors think in epochs rather than days or months.

The objective here is not romanticising slowness, but recognising time as an intentional asset class—something to be actively deployed, not passively endured. The lazy investor does less not for leisure, but because time itself amplifies the effect of prudent action. This philosophy values precision over passivity, depth over delay.

Time is not residual after a plan is drawn; it is the foundation upon which that plan must rest. When respected, it simplifies decision-making. When neglected, it renders every choice urgent. The investor who masters time—allocates it wisely, protects it fiercely, and trusts it fully—gains more than better returns. They gain something rarer: the quiet, compounding peace of mind that underpins not only wealth, but life itself.

The Forgotten Variable

In the architecture of most investment advice, time is mentioned often but understood poorly. It is referenced, nodded to, and occasionally revered, yet rarely treated as the primary design material. Asset allocation models highlight diversification. Risk tolerance questionnaires probe psychology. Portfolio reviews dwell on performance. But the most powerful variable—time—is almost always subordinated to what feels more tangible. This is a mistake not of ignorance, but of instinct. Time moves quietly. It offers no dashboard. It doesn't flash red. And because it whispers rather than shouts, most investors ignore it until it's too late.

This oversight is not accidental. Human psychology is fundamentally ill-suited to grasp exponential change. Our minds are wired for linear patterns, short feedback loops, and quick rewards. When we plant seeds, we look for sprouts the next day. When we save money, we check how much it has grown the next month. But investing does not yield its secrets on short horizons. Its rewards are not distributed evenly over time. They are *backloaded*—disproportionately delivered after long periods of compounding. And that makes time less intuitive, but *more essential.*

A lazy investor sees this not as a limitation, but as leverage. They understand that while money can be earned, lost, or borrowed—and risk can be managed, measured, or hedged—*time cannot be replaced.* It is the only asset that compounds without intervention. The only force that works harder the longer it is left alone. And the only variable that punishes meddling with ruthless precision. The lazy investor, then, is not passive out of apathy. They are inactive by design. They don't just tolerate time—they *engineer around it.*

The power of time in investing is exponential, not additive. To illustrate: £10,000 invested at 7% annual return becomes £20,000 in just over 10 years. In 20 years, it grows to nearly £40,000. But in 30 years, it balloons to over £76,000. The final decade adds more than the first two combined. This is not a quirk of arithmetic—it's the nature of compounding. Time is not neutral. It is *accelerative.* And the longer it is given, the more violently it bends the curve upwards. Investors who interrupt that curve with over-analysis, panic selling, or strategy changes are not just stepping sideways—they are *stepping off the compounding track entirely.*

This is what makes time such a misunderstood asset. It doesn't call attention to itself. It has no real-time metrics. But its impact dwarfs every other decision an investor makes. Asset allocation matters. Costs matter. Behaviour matters. But *time dominates.* Warren Buffett is not the wealthiest investor because he found the best returns—others have beaten him in performance—but because he started at age 10 and is still compounding in his 90s. His real secret is not brilliance. It is *duration.*

Why, then, do most investors fail to harness time properly? Because modern finance trains them to *distrust stillness.* We are flooded with market news, quarterly earnings, performance dashboards, and economic forecasts. Each data point implies urgency. Each fluctuation invites action. And each action, by extension, breaks the continuity that time requires to work its magic. Investors become addicted not to performance, but to feedback. They check, they adjust, they optimise—each move rationalised as diligence, when in truth it is often *disguised impatience.*

Here, the lazy investor introduces a countercultural stance: *Strategic detachment.* They recognise that trusting time requires more conviction than chasing returns. They build systems that can function unattended. Portfolios that do not need attention to perform. And mental models that resist the temptation to tinker. Their goal is not perfection in execution, but *consistency in intention.* They do not pretend to predict the future. They design portfolios that *don't need prediction to succeed*—just time.

One useful concept in this domain is the idea of "time arbitrage." Coined by investors like Charlie Munger and Howard Marks, it refers to the advantage gained simply by being willing to wait longer than others. In a market obsessed with quarterly performance, those who can extend their investment horizon to decades are playing a different game entirely. They are not competing on speed. They are compounding on endurance. And they win not because they act smarter, but because they *interrupt less.*

Consider the case of Terry Smith, manager of the Fundsmith Equity Fund. His philosophy is strikingly simple: buy high-quality businesses and hold them for a very long time. Over more than a decade, he has delivered top-tier returns not through innovation, but through *intentional boredom.* His turnover ratio is low. His communication is direct. And his results are a testament to what happens when time is left to run unmolested. Contrast this with investors who rotate sectors, time interest rates, or react to geopolitical headlines. Their portfolios may feel more dynamic—but over time, they are often *less effective.*

This is not to say that time alone guarantees success. It must be paired with a strategy robust enough to endure volatility, inflation, and behavioural pressure. But once that system is in place, *the most important skill becomes doing less.* This requires emotional training. Investors must learn to differentiate between *movement* and *progress.* Between *activity* and *advantage.* And most importantly, between *noise* and *signal.* Time amplifies whatever you feed into the system. Feed it discipline, and it rewards you. Feed it distraction, and it exposes you.

The laziness being advocated here is, therefore, not neglect. It is *selective engagement.* A refusal to squander time on low-value decisions. A conscious shift from being a manager of daily performance to a steward of long-term growth. The lazy investor thinks in decades, not days. They evaluate based on trajectory, not recent momentum. And they understand that wealth is not created by beating the market this week, but by *staying in the market long enough for time to do the heavy lifting.*

To bring this into sharper relief, consider how time interacts with mistakes. In most domains, errors are corrected quickly. You revise a paper. You iterate a design. But in investing, errors often *compound against you.* A poorly timed exit can erase years of gains. A reallocation done in fear can lock in losses. A chase after the "next big thing" can fragment a previously coherent portfolio. Time punishes these decisions not with immediate feedback, but with *opportunity cost that may take years to surface.* The lazy investor avoids this by *not needing to be right every time—only consistent enough to be right over time.*

This framing reorients the purpose of investment entirely. It moves us away from precision forecasting and toward probability stacking. It encourages a shift from maximising short-term alpha to maximising *time in the strategy*. The question becomes not "what will outperform this year?" but "what will still be valid in ten years?" That lens simplifies decision-making. It filters out the trendy, the tactical, the fragile. And it builds a relationship with money that is both more stable and more scalable.

Ultimately, time is not just an asset in the portfolio. It is the *force multiplier of every asset in the portfolio*. It turns adequacy into abundance. It turns restraint into results. And it turns lazy investing—not as in careless, but as in *committed to stillness*—into a legitimate edge. The most successful investors are not those who do the most. They are those who *interrupt the least*. Because every act of restraint extends the timeline. And every extension of the timeline increases the power of the one variable that can never be faked, outsourced, or shortcut.

Time is not the backdrop of investing. It is its *engine*. And the investor who sees that clearly—who honours it structurally, psychologically, and strategically—has already gained the most important advantage in finance: *alignment with the only force that guarantees compounding*. The rest is implementation. The real work is already done.

Compound Interest as a Spiritual Law

Most investors understand compound interest in purely financial terms: an arithmetic formula, a spreadsheet function, a by-product of time and return. They may even reference Einstein's alleged declaration of it as "the eighth wonder of the world," nodding to its raw numerical power. But what if compounding was not simply a mechanism of money growth, but a broader metaphor—*a philosophical lens through which to understand transformation itself*? What if the discipline required to unlock its financial rewards mirrored the psychological surrender required for deeper forms of personal evolution? Strip away the charts, the percentages, and the retirement calculators, and what remains is a spiritual principle hiding in plain sight: that growth comes not from force, but from patience; not from controlling outcomes, but from aligning with long-term processes and allowing them to unfold.

This is not a mystical reading of mathematics—it is a clarification of what compounding *actually asks of us*. At its core, compound interest is a reward for restraint. It is a system that punishes haste and honours stillness. The investor who trades compulsively, adjusts constantly, and insists on immediate progress sabotages the very mechanism they hope to harness. Conversely, the investor who sets a strategy, funds it with consistency, and resists the temptation to interfere is rewarded not only financially, but emotionally. They experience less turbulence, fewer regrets, and a quieter form of confidence that comes from being in sync with something larger than themselves. *This is what makes compounding spiritual: it asks you to relinquish control in order to receive abundance.*

In this sense, compounding echoes the teachings of multiple wisdom traditions. Consider the Taoist notion of *wu wei*—the principle of non-forcing, of effortlessness in alignment with nature. In the Tao Te Ching, Laozi writes, "Do you have the patience to wait till your mud settles and the water is clear?" Compounding is a form of *financial wu wei*. It does not reward busyness. It rewards *alignment with duration*. It asks that you plant and tend, then leave the soil undisturbed. The less you interfere, the more potent the result.

From a different angle, the Buddhist understanding of impermanence and mindfulness teaches that lasting outcomes emerge not from dramatic action but from consistent presence. Meditation, too, compounds. One session may feel trivial. Ten may feel difficult. But a hundred hours transforms the mind. Not through sudden insight, but through cumulative calibration. The long arc of investment behaves the same way. You don't wake up rich one morning. You wake up aligned, calm, and gradually freer—because you have chosen to trust in a process that outpaces your ability to monitor it in real time.

Even in Western philosophy, compounding resonates with classical notions of virtue. Aristotle viewed moral excellence not as a one-off achievement but as a habit built through repetition. Just as you become brave by acting bravely repeatedly, you become wealthy by *compounding disciplined decisions over time.* Both require faith in the invisible. Both resist shortcuts. And both collapse under erratic inputs.

This philosophical reframe matters because it changes the role of the investor from technician to participant in a longer, quieter unfolding. Instead of obsessing over marginal gains or optimal asset mixes, the lazy investor focuses on the *integrity of the system and the durability of their own behaviour within it.* They don't just believe in compounding as math. They honour it as a form of trust. And trust, as any spiritual tradition will tell you, is not passive—it is an active discipline. It requires us to resist the urge to interfere prematurely. It asks us to believe that things are working, even when they don't appear to be. It demands faith in the unseen.

This may sound impractical to some. Surely, they'll argue, investing is about data and diligence, not metaphysics. But consider the investors who outperform over 30 or 40 years. They are rarely the most reactive. They are almost never the most informed in any given year. What they do share is a set of behaviours that mirror spiritual practice: consistency, patience, detachment, humility, and perspective. They know that markets are noisy, that timing is impossible, and that ego is expensive. They therefore design systems that *do not require their constant attention.* They build portfolios they can *believe in enough to ignore.*

The key insight here is this: compound interest is not earned through intellect. It is earned through *temperament.* It is less about knowing what to do and more about resisting the impulse to undo it. Most investors fail not because they lack intelligence, but because they lack the emotional architecture to allow compounding to express itself. They withdraw at the wrong moment. They switch when patience is required. They respond to volatility by muting time's power, chasing the illusion of control. This is not a financial error. It is a spiritual one: the refusal to accept that some forces only work when left to unfold beyond our management.

That reframes risk entirely. Volatility, then, is not the greatest enemy. *Impatience is.* The lazy investor sees this clearly. They do not define success as "maximum return in minimum time." They define it as *resilience to temptation over long arcs.* That requires a kind of emotional engineering—one that builds buffers against impulse, space against reaction. It's why so many successful long-term investors automate their contributions, schedule infrequent portfolio reviews, and even restrict access to their brokerage accounts. These are not hacks. They are rituals. Systems designed to protect belief in compounding from the volatility of human behaviour.

Perhaps the most powerful real-world embodiment of this mindset is found in investors like John Bogle, the founder of Vanguard. Bogle's central idea—that you could achieve superior long-term results not by chasing returns but by owning the market and holding it indefinitely—was radical precisely because it sounded *too boring to be profitable.* But it worked. Not because of brilliance in selection, but because it respected time. His innovation was not financial. It was *philosophical.* He trusted compounding more than his own ability to outperform it.

In practical terms, the lesson here is deceptively simple: if you want exponential outcomes, you must design for surrender. Not passivity. Not ignorance. But *strategic surrender*—the conscious decision to place your energy not in constant evaluation, but in upfront configuration. To clarify your values, build your allocation, automate your actions, and then step back—not out of laziness, but because *you know the compound engine needs space to run.*

The irony is that the more effort you exert trying to "beat" compounding, the less likely you are to benefit from it. It's like trying to tug a tree into growing faster. You damage the roots. You interfere with the very mechanism that would've delivered fruit—had you let it. The lazy investor is wise not because they're disengaged, but because *they know where their attention is most valuable.* They invest their energy in building durable systems, and then withdraw their ego from the outcome.

This is what makes compound interest a spiritual law: it transforms not just wealth, but worldview. It teaches patience not as resignation, but as power. It elevates stillness as strategy. And it rewards those who can detach from urgency in favour of duration. That is no longer a financial idea. It is a life principle. A way of navigating not just markets, but relationships, careers, health, and self-development. Anything worthwhile compounds. And everything that compounds asks us to *stay out of the way* just long enough for the process to surpass our ability to predict it.

To view compound interest in this light is to see investing not as a game of outperformance, but as a practice of surrender. A choice to align with time rather than try to outmanoeuvre it. The payoff, of course, is not just financial freedom. It's psychological freedom: the ability to step back, observe, and rest in the knowledge that *stillness can be strategy.* That sometimes, *the most powerful thing you can do is nothing at all.*

The Patience Premium:

Every investor believes they're patient—until the market tests them. Amid the hum of news cycles, portfolio dashboards, and minute-by-minute price alerts, the discipline to do nothing has become an extraordinary form of action. While modern finance measures risk, volatility, and returns down to three decimal places, it rarely quantifies the value of time held quietly. Yet, paradoxically, this quiet—this restraint—is where the deepest rewards accrue. *The market does not pay for activity; it pays for abstention in the face of noise.* That premium—the difference between those who wait and those who react—is not incidental. It is the very heart of how wealth compounds.

Behavioural economists have long observed that humans are poorly wired for delayed gratification. From the marshmallow tests of the 1960s to modern neuroeconomic research, the evidence is overwhelming: we vastly prefer the certainty of now over the uncertainty of later. In markets, this translates into action bias—trading too often, rebalancing too early, selling too soon. But every study of long-term wealth creation returns to the same truth: the longer you hold quality assets, the greater your odds of not just positive returns—but *asymmetrically outsized* ones.

Consider the empirical findings from Morningstar's "Mind the Gap" reports, which consistently show a striking behavioural penalty: the average investor underperforms the funds they invest in—often by 1 to 1.5% annually—simply because they buy high, sell low, and chase performance. This is not a gap of intelligence or access. It is a gap of impulse. Patience doesn't just preserve returns; it recaptures them from our own psychological sabotage.

This isn't theoretical. Let's take a concrete example. Between 1994 and 2022, the S&P 500 returned approximately 9.7% per annum. But if you missed just the 10 best days over those 28 years—days which are virtually impossible to predict in advance—your annual return dropped to just 5.5%. Miss the best 30 days, and you're barely outperforming inflation. What's extraordinary is that these "best days" often occur in close proximity to the worst ones. The temptation to sell during turbulence often strips investors of their right to enjoy the recovery. *The cost of impatience isn't just lost opportunity—it's statistically baked into the very fabric of underperformance.*

Now layer onto that a second phenomenon: the endurance of long-dated compounding. Imagine two investors: one who earns 7% annually over 20 years, and another who earns 7% annually over 30 years. The second investor isn't 50% wealthier—she's more than twice as rich. That extra decade doesn't add value linearly; it magnifies it exponentially. What's invisible in year five becomes undeniable in year fifteen. And yet, the ability to stay the course across decades is not a product of IQ, forecasting skill, or algorithmic advantage—it's the result of temperament, design, and time orientation.

This is where the concept of the "patience premium" becomes philosophically powerful. The market may fluctuate randomly in the short term, but it reliably rewards one behaviour: *the disciplined act of waiting*. And importantly, waiting is not passive. It requires structural foresight. To hold through volatility, one must first construct a portfolio that is psychologically survivable. This means selecting allocations not just for theoretical risk-adjusted returns, but for emotional endurance. A high-returning strategy is worthless if the investor cannot stick with it.

This is also why the lazy investor, paradoxically, is often the most resilient. Because their system is designed for disengagement—not out of neglect, but out of respect for compounding. They do not confuse movement with progress. Their aim is not excitement, but *continuity*. They earn their returns the way nature grows forests: steadily, cyclically, and imperceptibly—until one day, the outcome is too vast to ignore.

Of course, critics argue that markets are different now—more volatile, more global, more driven by algorithmic trading and geopolitical shocks. And that's partially true. But the noise has always changed; the signal hasn't. Market regimes shift, sentiment cycles evolve, crises erupt. But the consistent differentiator between wealth creation and erosion remains: *time in the market trumps timing the market.*

We can even observe this premium cross-culturally. Consider the strategies of sovereign wealth funds like Norway's Government Pension Fund Global. With over $1 trillion in assets, it is managed not for quarterly outperformance but for generational stability. Its mandate? To invest with a horizon of 30 to 50 years. Likewise, institutions like the Yale Endowment, under the late David Swensen, built extraordinary long-term returns by leaning into illiquid, high-conviction positions that demanded—and rewarded—patience. These models don't require clairvoyance. They require conviction in *staying put.*

Yet if patience is so clearly valuable, why is it so rare? The answer lies not in the markets, but in ourselves. We are emotional creatures in a digital age of constant comparison. Every day, we are flooded with portfolio updates, pundit forecasts, fintech alerts, and index trackers. Our time horizons are measured in hours, not years. Even the most rational investor must now work to *protect their attention span as a financial asset.*

This is where intentional tools become essential. A "default investment system"—automated contributions, rules-based allocations, and pre-scheduled rebalancing—acts as a buffer against over-engagement. It creates friction against fiddling. And perhaps more subtly, it invites the investor to reimagine their role—not as a daily manager of outcomes, but as a patient cultivator of long-term tendencies.

There's also a psychological reframing required: to associate *peace* with non-action, rather than fear. Most investors struggle not because they lack a plan, but because they don't trust it enough to leave it alone. They confuse vigilance with control. But just as watching a seed obsessively doesn't make it sprout faster, monitoring a portfolio hourly does not compound it more efficiently. In fact, it does the opposite—it tempts unnecessary intervention.

To internalise the patience premium is to accept a certain humility: that markets will misbehave, that one cannot master them day to day, and that the most elegant strategy may be one that asks less of you, not more. It is to shift from performance anxiety to process alignment. To prioritise the *probability* of wealth over the *possibility* of excitement.

Ultimately, the patience premium is not a secret tactic or hidden arbitrage. It is the natural reward of emotional discipline, structural design, and temporal orientation. It asks the investor a simple question: *Can you wait longer than others without needing to prove that you're right along the way?* Those who can, often don't just outperform. They outlast.

And in investing, that is everything.

The Decade Decision Rule:

The average investor wakes up with the markets. They check headlines, monitor fluctuations, chase narratives, and pivot portfolios based on movements so small they'd be indistinguishable from noise under any long-term lens. The emotional cadence of this behaviour feels like diligence—but it's not. It's distraction disguised as discipline. The most consistent investment advantage rarely comes from doing more. It comes from seeing further. That is the essence of the Decade Decision Rule: act today in ways that will make sense ten years from now—not ten days. In a world calibrated to instant gratification and algorithmic feedback loops, zooming out is no longer a luxury. It's a competitive edge.

Consider the paradox: markets are long-term voting machines for value, yet investor behaviour is overwhelmingly short-termist. Portfolio shifts are rationalised with sophisticated jargon—rebalancing, risk calibration, macro positioning—but many stem from a myopic discomfort with stillness. That discomfort is expensive. Morningstar data consistently shows that the returns investors earn are lower than the returns their funds generate. This gap—aptly named the "behaviour gap"—is not due to a lack of intellect or access. It's the product of reactive decision-making. Investors bail at the bottom, buy after rallies, and over-customise in pursuit of certainty. The Decade Decision Rule offers a counterweight: a mental framework to enforce patience by design, not by personality.

The rule is elegantly simple. Before executing any financial decision—whether it's buying a stock, rebalancing a portfolio, shifting asset classes, or adjusting a retirement plan—ask one question: *Will this still make sense ten years from now?* If the answer depends on short-term conditions, recent news, or "timing the cycle," that's your cue to pause. The rule forces alignment between action and time horizon. Most investing errors occur when the behaviour horizon shrinks faster than the asset horizon. You hold a thirty-year asset but act like you're managing a thirty-day risk.

This discipline matters because most of the rewards in investing come not from brilliance but from duration. A mediocre portfolio held for a decade often outperforms a brilliant one shuffled every few months. This isn't an argument against intelligence; it's an argument for restraint. Markets rarely reward the most clever. They reward the most consistent. And consistency is easier when your decisions are filtered through a decade-sized lens.

Zooming out also restores proportion. Short-term volatility becomes noise, not signal. Bear markets become seasons, not disasters. Sector rotations and headlines lose their urgency. A ten-year view transforms the question from "What's happening right now?" to "What do I want compounding quietly in the background as life happens?" Suddenly, the investor becomes less of a trader and more of a designer—curating a system that fits not just a risk profile but a life philosophy.

Historical data strongly supports this perspective. Take the S&P 500 as a proxy. In any given one-day period, the market has a slightly better than 50% chance of being up. Over one year, the odds of gain rise to about 75%. Over any rolling ten-year period since the 1920s, the probability of a positive return has hovered above 90%. This asymmetry rewards time, not timing. The longer your lens, the fewer decisions you need to make—and the better your odds of success. The Decade Decision Rule simply gives that insight structure.

It's also worth noting what the rule doesn't do. It doesn't guarantee outcomes. It doesn't eliminate uncertainty. And it doesn't exempt you from risk. What it does is enforce a kind of mental hygiene—a prophylactic against emotional overreach. Like a constitutional clause for your financial behaviour, it protects long-term logic from short-term temptation. It's not about being passive. It's about being principled.

One compelling example comes from the tech entrepreneur-turned-investor Naval Ravikant, who has spoken frequently about his preference for bets that compound over decades. He frames time as the ultimate arbitrage: most people can't wait. If you can, you win. In a podcast, he described wealth not as income but as ownership—of assets that increase in value without requiring your presence. The key, he argued, was to choose carefully, act slowly, and then *do nothing* for as long as possible. It's a strategy that sounds like laziness, but in practice requires profound discipline. The Decade Decision Rule operationalises that ethos.

There's a deeper philosophical elegance here too. The rule embraces uncertainty not as a flaw to be fixed but as a feature to be respected. You don't need to predict the next recession, the next rate hike, or the next headline. You only need to ensure that your decisions would still hold water if looked at from the vantage point of 2035. That standard eliminates a wide range of speculative errors. It strips away ego. It demands coherence between your values and your capital. And it rewards a rare form of wisdom: knowing that you don't need to know everything today.

But how does one apply this practically? Begin with your portfolio design. If your allocation would not make sense to your future self—either because it's too fragile, too complex, or too dependent on regular tinkering—it's probably not sustainable. The same principle applies to spending decisions. Ask whether your current consumption choices reflect your ten-year ambitions. Are you financing temporary status or enduring freedom? Time spent with this rule will often expose not just financial inefficiencies but philosophical drift.

Even outside traditional investing, the Decade Decision Rule proves versatile. In career choices, for example, short-term incentives (a promotion, a raise, a title) often drive moves that, in hindsight, yield diminishing returns. A decade filter clarifies whether a job, a business, or even a partnership is directionally aligned with your deeper values. It sharpens the distinction between velocity and trajectory.

Critically, this mental model also deflates urgency. Much of modern finance is structured to make you feel behind. The news cycle, the notification loop, the performance scoreboard—they all manufacture immediacy. The Decade Decision Rule counters this with deliberate slowness. It says: *You're not late. You're early—if you're willing to wait.* This reframing is not just strategic; it's emotional. It gives you permission to detach, observe, and design a financial life rooted in clarity, not clutter.

None of this implies that you should never act. It simply demands that when you do act, the rationale must pass a far stricter test than most investors apply. Imagine being interviewed by your future self. Would you be able to defend the decision convincingly? Would the logic still hold in a changed world? If not, you're probably chasing performance, not building permanence.

The lazy investor, as this book argues, is not idle. They are intentional. They understand that the compounding of capital is indifferent to activity. It thrives on aligned, durable, well-spaced decisions. The Decade Decision Rule is one of the most effective behavioural anchors for this mindset. It removes the illusion of control. It centres time as your ally. And it repositions patience not as passive virtue, but as active design.

Ultimately, adopting the Decade Decision Rule is less about reducing risk than about reducing regret. Few investors look back and lament waiting. Many regret rushing. A system designed around decade-long coherence avoids the psychological whiplash of reactive investing. It doesn't promise excitement. But it offers something rarer: calm clarity in a world obsessed with motion.

That clarity is your advantage. It's how you stay still while the world spins, and still move forward faster than most. That's not just smart investing. It's wise living.

Chapter 6
Automation and Its Emotional Gifts

For all the chatter about wealth creation, most investing literature quietly misses the point: the real challenge is rarely selecting the right assets, but enduring yourself while they compound. Markets reward consistency; the human mind, by contrast, craves stimulation. Pattern recognition, emotion, novelty—all these drive behaviour in ways that conflict with steady accumulation. Investing, at its best, should feel dull. Yet our brains are addicted to checking, tweaking, second-guessing. Properly conceived automation is more than convenience—it is an emotional intervention. It interrupts the loop between attention and action, shielding us from our own impulses.

This chapter is not a catalogue of apps or algorithms. It is about designing freedom. Real automation is philosophical, not merely mechanical. It is the art of pre-deciding, of constructing systems so well aligned with long-term objectives that you can forget them—without guilt, doubt, or lingering anxiety. Automation becomes a declaration of trust in your future self: disciplined, wise, and deserving of serenity.

"Set it and forget it" has been trivialised over decades, but its essence remains revolutionary. It promised a world in which commitment could be codified and execution insulated from the whims of mood or market noise. Yet many investors never reach that state—not because the tools are lacking, but because their psychology resists it. Systems are installed, but mistrusted. Contributions automated, yet obsessively monitored. Portfolios outsourced, yet scrutinised compulsively. The machinery runs quietly, but anxiety stays front and centre.

Here, automation is reframed as an emotional discipline. It is not mere delegation; it is deliberate disentanglement. To benefit fully, reactive behaviours must be replaced with intentional rituals. This is not abdication; it is foresight. A bridge does not require constant inspection to remain standing; a well-designed investment system does not require perpetual supervision. But such a system demands rigour upfront, followed by conscious withdrawal.

We begin with clarity: what should be automated? Obvious answers—monthly contributions, rebalancing, dividend reinvestment—are only the surface. Deeper automation addresses behavioural triggers, threshold-based alerts, scheduled "ignore" periods, and pre-defined rules for turbulent markets. Each replaces a potential emotional decision with a pre-installed mechanism. Done well, the system operates psychologically as well as logically, removing options for overreaction.

Consider the investor who funds their index portfolio monthly via standing order. Mechanically, this is effective. Yet if they spend the remaining days monitoring returns obsessively, reading commentary, or debating allocations, the emotional architecture remains exposed. True automation closes the loop, directing behaviour and easing the mind.

The most powerful systems confer emotional spaciousness. This is the overlooked dividend of automation: practical peace. The ability to sleep through a correction, to go weeks without checking, to trust that goals are progressing even in absence of attention. This is not laziness—it is stewardship.

We explore three intertwined frameworks. First, the mechanical: deploying tools—from robo-advisors to algorithmic rebalancers—effectively. Second, the behavioural: crafting rituals that replace noise with clarity, such as the "One-Hour Annual Check-In," condensing a year of low-value monitoring into a single session of focused assessment. Third, the emotional: reinforcing trust in your system so detachment feels confident, not neglectful.

Trusting the system you built is often the hardest task. Many investors are brilliant engineers but poor stewards. They understand allocation models and optimisation algorithms, yet still feel exposed. Automation without internalisation is fragile; doubt leads to peeking, peeking leads to interference, and interference erodes compounding.

We examine strategies to cultivate trust: decision journaling to preserve reasoning, deliberate detachment periods to resist unnecessary action, and design principles that align emotion with process. Without internalised confidence, automation merely defers stress rather than eliminating it.

Systems thinking is central. Drawing from software architecture, industrial design, and behavioural economics, we construct what might be called a money machine—a repeatable, low-maintenance engine for long-term wealth. This is not about chasing annual returns; it is about maximising lifetime emotional utility. The true ROI of automation is measured in mental bandwidth reclaimed, not basis points gained.

A system that allows you to sleep is more than convenient—it is dignified. It honours your time, attention, and future. Automation should feel like integrity, not outsourcing: the actions of your present self aligned with your future needs, even when absent. That is the highest standard of investment design: functionality in your presence is expected; functionality in your absence is mastery.

Chapter Six reframes automation not as technical sophistication, but as a philosophy of deliberate disengagement. Disengagement here does not imply negligence; it signifies maturity—the confidence to avoid proving oneself daily. It is the art of designing a system that grows quietly in the background, freeing your mind to live. The result is not merely compounding capital, but compounding peace. That is the ultimate gift of automation, and it deserves careful construction.

Set It and Forget It—For Real:

Most people don't invest; they micromanage. What passes for strategy is often just a disguised state of perpetual monitoring—adjusting allocations on a whim, tweaking inputs in response to headlines, interpreting volatility as personal feedback. Yet paradoxically, almost every credible study of long-term investment performance points to the same truth: *the less you do, the better you tend to fare.* This is not merely because inactivity avoids mistakes. It's because consistent, disciplined inaction in the presence of temptation is itself the behaviour most correlated with wealth creation.

Automation, then, is not just a convenience—it is a philosophical commitment to the idea that long-term investing should remove the human impulse to tinker. To *set it and forget it* is not laziness. It is design. It reflects a recognition that the investor's worst enemy is not poor information, but surplus attention.

The modern investor has no excuse for failing to automate. The infrastructure is already in place. Scheduled bank transfers, automated index fund contributions, algorithmic portfolio rebalancing, dividend reinvestment plans, and tax-harvesting services are no longer exotic—they are standard. What remains uncommon is the willingness to *trust* these tools to do their work uninterrupted. The average person uses automation to execute tasks but still insists on watching over them, hovering, doubting, and occasionally overriding the very system they built. This is not automation. It is surveillance in disguise.

To make automation effective, it must *intervene in behaviour*, not merely logistics. Setting up an automatic contribution is only valuable if you no longer treat each market dip as a referendum on your previous decisions. The goal is not just to save time—it is to reclaim emotional bandwidth. When systems take over function, they should also relieve *friction.* If they don't, they are incomplete.

There is a subtle difference between automation as an act of convenience and automation as a design principle. The former solves a time problem; the latter solves a trust problem. Convenience-based automation says, "I'll let the system handle this while I'm busy." Design-based automation says, "I'll let the system handle this *because I should never be involved in the first place.*" This distinction is vital. Investors who automate for convenience tend to intervene when discomfort arises. Investors who automate by design don't. Their emotional contract is different.

This is where most automation strategies fall short. They reduce the number of manual steps but leave the investor emotionally exposed. A scheduled contribution helps, but it doesn't stop the investor from wondering every few weeks whether the market is "too high" to buy in. Rebalancing software ensures target allocations are maintained, but it doesn't insulate against the fear of underperformance during strong rallies in more aggressive assets. The systems are present—but untrusted.

True automation involves *psychological offboarding*. The investor must understand and accept *why* the system is better than they are. This isn't about self-deprecation. It's about recognising structural mismatch: our brains are built for short-term survival; markets reward long-term patience. Automation is the reconciliation of those two realities.

This requires us to redefine what success looks like. For decades, investing has been taught as a performance contest. Sharpe ratios, alpha, risk-adjusted returns—all legitimate metrics, but ones that encourage comparative anxiety. Automation offers an alternative measure: *how little attention did this require from me to succeed?* That is the key indicator for the lazy investor. Not how clever the strategy was, but how invisible it became.

The emotional benefits of this redefinition are enormous. When your system is humming quietly in the background—executing contributions, rebalancing, allocating—your mental space clears. You don't need to check whether you're "on track" every week. You don't need to stress about macro forecasts or central bank statements. You've installed the engine. Now you just keep fuelling it. This simplicity liberates. It turns investing from a constant negotiation with uncertainty into a periodic act of reinforcement.

Let's be clear: good automation is front-loaded discipline. It requires thoughtful planning, clear parameters, and a rigorous understanding of the strategy. But once deployed, it must be protected from interference. That means creating barriers to entry—deliberately making it *harder* to intervene impulsively. In practice, this could involve setting up accounts you don't log into frequently, using financial custodians that prevent same-day trading, or creating "cool-down periods" before making any portfolio change. These are not technological tricks. They are emotional safeguards.

Robo-advisors exemplify this model. They ask the investor to define their goals and risk profile *once*, and then execute continuously against that blueprint—no prompting, no panic. Yet even here, investors tend to underperform the systems they use. Why? Because they override them. When the market falls, they reduce risk. When it rises, they chase momentum. The automation succeeds technically but fails emotionally. The problem was never the algorithm—it was the user's belief that they could improve it with anxiety-driven inputs.

Scheduled transfers are another core automation tool. They embody the principle of *deliberate indifference*—money flows from your income into your investment vehicle regardless of what the headlines say. This creates a time-weighted exposure to the market that eliminates guesswork. But more importantly, it eliminates decision fatigue. Every unscheduled investment requires a choice: "Now?" Every choice invites a narrative. Every narrative is a potential error. The scheduled transfer removes the entire chain.

At scale, these mechanisms begin to construct what we might call an *emotional firewall*—a set of systems that insulate the investor not just from bad decisions, but from the stress of constant re-evaluation. The portfolio becomes something you check on occasion, but rarely think about. It does not compete with your work, your family, your health, or your creativity for mental real estate. It simply grows.

Critics sometimes argue that automation promotes complacency. But the opposite is true. Automation is an act of *proactive intention.* It requires more thinking up front and less meddling later. It is not the investor who automates that is negligent, but the one who relies on ad hoc decisions under pressure. The truth is that most people are already on autopilot—they are just on *bad* autopilot. They react to noise. They chase trends. They follow fear. Real automation replaces this chaos with design.

To that end, the automation you implement should be both mechanical and reflective. It should perform functions *and* reinforce beliefs. A system that executes contributions and rebalances allocations is effective. But a system that also reminds you, passively and repeatedly, that *you don't need to touch this*—that's transformative. That is how automation becomes a source of calm rather than simply a background task.

This reframing opens a deeper insight: automation is not just about reducing effort. It is about *designing identity*. The investor who no longer checks their balance every week is not just saving time—they are becoming the kind of person who does not require reassurance from fluctuation. They are cultivating emotional resilience through architectural choice. Over time, this rewires their relationship with money itself.

So, what does it mean to "set it and forget it—for real"? It means you design a system that works *without you*. You define it once, inspect it occasionally, and resist the urge to improve it in response to emotion. You stop trying to outsmart markets, and start trying to out-discipline your future self. You embrace boredom, because it means the machine is running. You give up control, and in doing so, you gain peace.

In the end, automation is not the enemy of control. It is the highest expression of it. It says: I have thought deeply about what matters. I have built something that reflects those priorities. And now, I will get out of its way. That's not passive. That's mastery.

When Ritual Replaces Reaction:

The allure of real-time information is both modern and primal. Investors now reach for their phones with the same frequency and reflex as one checks the time or scrolls social media. But this habit—daily, hourly, sometimes compulsively—is not born of insight-seeking. It is a nervous tic, an emotional hedge against uncertainty. The irony is sharp: while the data available to investors has exploded in volume and immediacy, emotional stability has diminished in equal measure. *We are watching more, knowing less, and sleeping worse.*

At the heart of this behavioural dissonance is a fundamental error: confusing activity with control. Many investors believe that constant vigilance is synonymous with being a responsible steward of capital. They monitor markets like air traffic controllers, scanning for threats, alerts, and anomalies. But unlike planes, portfolios don't need to be landed every day. In fact, they perform best when left alone. *The human impulse to monitor becomes the very source of underperformance—financially and psychologically.*

This subchapter argues for a radical reorientation. The goal is not to eliminate discipline but to *recode it.* What if the antidote to reactivity was not ignorance, but *ritual?* What if detachment didn't mean laziness, but design?

The transition from reaction to ritual begins by understanding that most financial behaviours are not driven by data but by discomfort. Uncertainty is an evolutionary stressor. In markets, it manifests as the temptation to do *something.* Check. Adjust. Hedge. Rebalance. Even if no action is taken, the constant peeking inflates the emotional cost of investing. Studies show that frequent portfolio monitoring reduces reported happiness—even during bull markets. The more often we check, the more often we encounter volatility, even if it's meaningless noise. Like measuring your height every morning, the fluctuations are statistically inevitable and practically irrelevant—but they distort self-perception and invite premature intervention.

The behavioural finance literature is unambiguous here. Daniel Kahneman's work on *loss aversion* suggests that losses feel twice as painful as equivalent gains feel rewarding. If you're checking your portfolio daily, you're far more likely to witness paper losses—even in an upward-trending market. These losses trigger cortisol responses, reduce decision quality, and foster the illusion that the system is broken when it's simply following its design. *The problem is not the market; it's the microscope.*

Replacing reaction with ritual requires installing a set of predictable, low-friction behaviours that absorb our need for control without compromising strategic detachment. One such ritual, deceptively simple in concept and profound in implication, is what I call the *One-Hour Annual Check-In.* Done correctly, it compresses the emotional cost of investing into a single, bounded, intentional moment.

The check-in is not a performance review. It is not an invitation to fiddle. It is a structured reaffirmation. Once a year—at the same time, on the same date—you review the fundamentals: Are my goals still the same? Has my timeline changed? Have I experienced a life event that warrants reassessment? If the answer is no, you change nothing. You remind yourself that this portfolio was built not for this month or this news cycle, but for a 20-year horizon. You log out. You go live your life.

For those who feel this is too infrequent—who protest, "But what if the market crashes?"—it's useful to invert the logic. Most investors should ask, "What if my reactions cause the damage?" History is littered with data showing that market crashes are rarely the primary destroyer of wealth; *panic exits during crashes* are. In other words, *emotion, not the event, is the risk.*

Let's be precise: rituals are not the absence of discipline—they are the automation of it. Rituals safeguard our attention from the illusion that more observation equals better outcomes. In fact, many of the world's most disciplined investors are the least active. Vanguard founder Jack Bogle famously advocated for what he called the "stay-the-course" mentality. His personal investment strategy, even with unmatched access to data and insight, was to rebalance occasionally and ignore the news. His returns didn't suffer for it—his *sanity* benefitted. Rituals create this separation: between what the market is doing, and what you need to do.

A core emotional benefit of ritual is what psychologists call *cognitive offloading.* When you know that you'll review your finances at a pre-scheduled, dedicated time, the need to repeatedly interrogate the portfolio diminishes. It's the same reason that writing down a to-do list helps reduce anxiety—not because the tasks are done, but because the brain trusts they won't be forgotten. Rituals work similarly: *they install a floor of trust beneath your attention.*

Critically, the ritual must be minimal, consistent, and untempting. The reason so many financial apps and dashboards induce anxiety is not just their content but their *design.* They are built to spike engagement and provoke checking. A ritual, by contrast, is structured to *contain* curiosity, not stimulate it. If your ritual requires more than a calendar alert, a cup of coffee, and an hour of calm, it's probably too elaborate. Discipline that is hard to do is discipline that will fail. *Lazy must mean low-friction, not low-intention.*

It's worth emphasising that reaction is not just a behaviour—it's a worldview. It's the belief that the more involved you are, the safer you are. But wealth building is not war. It's not a contest of vigilance. It's farming, not hunting. It rewards patience, not precision. The shift from reaction to ritual is a philosophical one: *it affirms that doing less can be done with more clarity, more intent, and better results.*

This shift has neurological consequences as well. The reward systems in the brain—especially those governed by dopamine—respond differently to uncertainty than to mastery. Reacting to every blip in your portfolio keeps the brain in a loop of partial reinforcement: unpredictable, inconsistent outcomes that reinforce addictive checking. By contrast, a ritual, especially one tied to clear boundaries and predictable timing, retrains the dopamine system to seek validation from discipline, not novelty. *Ritual becomes its own reward.*

Let's return to the central metaphor of the "One-Hour Annual Check-In." This is not a tactical gimmick. It is a strategic boundary. It is the assertion that *peace is the performance.* The market doesn't care how often you look. The more you can detach your sense of competence from the frequency of your involvement, the closer you move toward a healthier relationship with money. And relationships—emotional, financial, or otherwise—are not improved by hovering. They are strengthened by trust.

For investors who wish to go further, the ritual can also serve as an opportunity for gratitude. Not in a naïve or sentimental way, but in a reflective, data-driven way: look at your long-term trajectory. Acknowledge the distance between panic and plan. Recognise that if your portfolio is boring, that's a feature. *The best systems are not stimulating—they're forgettable.*

By codifying reaction into ritual, the investor upgrades from an anxious observer to a calm architect. You stop responding to noise and start responding to need. And you do it once a year, not once an hour.

If that sounds radical, good. It means you've finally started to measure wealth not just in returns—but in *attention reclaimed.*

Building the Money Machine:

The prevailing myth in personal finance is that wealth is earned through consistent hustle, constant attention, and finely tuned responses to every market twitch. Yet the investors who end up quietly winning—those who sleep better, worry less, and ultimately accumulate more—often do the opposite. They build machines, not obsessions. They think in systems, not spreadsheets. They engineer flow, not friction. And most critically, they structure their financial lives to run with minimal intervention. The lazy investor, far from being negligent, is the one who invests the most up front—in architecture, not anxiety.

The concept of a "money machine" might sound mechanistic or even gimmicky at first glance. But when we strip it down, the phrase simply refers to a system that can repeatedly convert income into wealth without requiring constant decision-making. This is not about passive income in the over-marketed, clickbait sense. It's about *systematised momentum*—a design that channels earnings, automates allocation, and insulates execution from emotion. Like a well-designed piece of software, the goal is not perfection but reliability under imperfect conditions. The system works because it doesn't need your daily attention to function.

Systems thinking, borrowed from engineering and biology, is built on one core idea: *structure determines behaviour.* Most people fail financially not due to lack of intelligence or effort, but because they operate within systems that sabotage them. They rely on willpower, not design. They spend energy resisting temptation instead of removing it. By contrast, the financially unbothered investor sets up flows—automatic transfers, scheduled investments, fixed allocation rules—that eliminate the need to choose every month. When your structure is sound, your discipline becomes irrelevant.

To build a durable financial machine, the first design principle is *default automation.* This means removing human discretion from recurring financial decisions. Income hits your account? A fixed percentage routes immediately to investments. Markets go up or down? Your contribution doesn't change. The same ETF, the same date, the same amount. You could be on a flight, in a meeting, or asleep—and your wealth engine continues humming. Importantly, this is not a form of neglect. It's a form of trust. *Automation is not laziness. It's pre-approved wisdom.*

Consider the design elegance of a basic money pipeline: salary arrives → automatic deduction to investment account → auto-purchase of diversified fund. The system might be three steps, but its implications are enormous. It removes timing stress, decision fatigue, and the tendency to over-optimise based on recent headlines. This is what Daniel Kahneman might call *noise reduction.* A cleaner signal, fewer decisions, better outcomes.

The lazy investor does not simply abdicate responsibility—they front-load it. The time they don't spend checking markets or tweaking spreadsheets is time they already spent months ago selecting robust index funds, writing down a clear investment policy, and aligning their contributions with long-term targets. The machine was built before it was needed. This principle mirrors software engineering's "You Aren't Gonna Need It" doctrine: build only what's essential, but make it stable. Investing systems are not meant to be beautiful or complex; they're meant to be anti-fragile. The best systems survive boredom.

Nowhere is this more evident than in portfolio allocation. The conventional investor might reactively rebalance based on fear or greed, shifting between asset classes in response to noise. But the machine-builder selects an allocation—say, 60% global equities, 30% bonds, 10% alternatives—and automates rebalancing semi-annually. This structure does not optimise for excitement. It optimises for consistency. More importantly, it removes the investor from the equation at the moment their judgement is most compromised—during volatility.

The machine mindset also reconfigures the way we perceive effort. High-maintenance investing often masquerades as sophistication, yet more activity rarely correlates with better results. In fact, over-management is statistically punished. Studies from Vanguard, Fidelity, and independent behavioural economists have consistently shown that portfolios with fewer interventions tend to outperform—not due to brilliance, but due to the absence of costly mistakes. *Effort, in investing, does not scale linearly with reward.* The more you touch the system, the more you risk contaminating it.

The key to machine-building is embracing boredom as a feature, not a flaw. A well-structured financial system should become uninteresting over time. If it excites you weekly, something is likely wrong. The machine should not solicit your attention. If anything, your engagement should decline as the system matures. This is a hard psychological shift for high-achievers. Many professionals struggle with the idea that something important—like wealth—can be left alone. But just as a well-built bridge doesn't need daily adjustments to stay upright, a well-built investment system thrives on inattention.

Of course, machines must be tested. Trust does not precede reliability—it follows it. That's why periodic calibration is necessary, but it should be structured. The one-hour annual check-in, introduced in the next section, serves this function. A fixed date, a fixed process, a fixed duration. No spontaneous tinkering, no stress-based interference. Just a system audit: Are contributions flowing? Is allocation within range? Are fees still low? This ritualistic review reinforces the structure without destabilising it.

Systems thinking also requires designing for friction—not eliminating it entirely, but placing it *strategically*. For example, placing your investment account at a different bank from your current account introduces a small obstacle to withdrawal. This minor speed bump can prevent impulsive moves. It's what behavioural economists call a *commitment device*—a design feature that protects you from your future, weaker self. Systems are not just about flow; they're about resistance in the right places.

To fully benefit from the money machine approach, the investor must learn to separate outcomes from appearances. A system that feels "too simple" might be working precisely because it avoids unnecessary complexity. If your investments look like they run on autopilot, that's not a failure of engagement; it's a triumph of design. *Clarity is the true sophistication.* The lazy investor is not disengaged from finance because they don't care. They're disengaged because they've already done the caring—in advance, deliberately, and systemically.

Ultimately, building the money machine is not just a financial act—it's a philosophical one. It reflects a belief in structure over spontaneity, in discipline by design rather than discipline by force. It accepts that human attention is finite and fallible, and uses that humility to create a system that can endure without it. In a culture that glorifies optimisation, the machine is a quiet rebellion. It says: I don't need to win every day. I just need to keep working, even when I'm not.

That's not laziness. That's leverage.

Trusting the Machine You Built:

Perhaps the most paradoxical moment in building a robust investment system is what follows its completion—not relief, but resistance. You've done the research, chosen the allocation, automated the transfers, clarified your rebalancing schedule, and documented your principles. The infrastructure is in place. The machine is operational. And yet, something in you hesitates. This is not a technical failure. It's emotional reluctance. Trusting the machine you've built demands a shift from control to conviction—from tweaking inputs to tolerating stillness. For many, this is the hardest part of all.

The modern investor is conditioned to believe that vigilance equals virtue. Watchfulness, we are told, is synonymous with responsibility. The idea of stepping away—of letting a system run without daily human oversight—feels not only unnatural, but negligent. This mindset is understandable but ultimately misplaced. In investing, constant supervision often erodes returns rather than protects them. *The machine works best not when you optimise it constantly, but when you leave it alone.*

This is not an argument for blind faith. Quite the opposite. True trust is not ignorance; it's earned confidence. And confidence in a system arises from two places: knowing how it works, and having proof that it works. In other words, trust is built at the intersection of understanding and evidence. You must design systems that are not only functional, but *comprehensible*—simple enough to be explainable, yet strong enough to be resilient.

To cultivate this trust, one of the most effective techniques is what might be called *retrospective calibration.* This involves running historical simulations—not for predictive certainty, but for emotional inoculation. What would your current system have done in 2008? In 2020? During the dot-com crash or the bull run of the 2010s? Seeing your portfolio allocation hold, recover, and compound through volatile periods provides a visceral grounding. It turns theory into trust. It reminds you that *systems don't avoid turbulence—they absorb it.*

But simulations are not enough. The next layer of trust-building is *personal conviction through documentation.* This is where your Investment Policy Statement (IPS) becomes a psychological anchor. If written thoughtfully, your IPS should articulate not only what you're doing, but *why*—your principles, your timelines, your risk tolerance, your non-negotiables. When the market is calm, this document may feel redundant. When it's stormy, it becomes your compass. It externalises your rational self, so that your reactive self has something to return to.

Still, even with simulations and written principles, doubt will creep in—particularly in long periods of flat or declining performance. This is where trust becomes less a function of intellect and more one of practice. *Discipline is not the absence of emotion; it's the muscle that keeps you from acting on it.* One powerful exercise here is the *scheduled permission check.* Once per quarter—or even once per year—give yourself permission to review your system with full scrutiny. But outside of that window, you do nothing. No logging in, no reallocating, no reacting. You are not suppressing curiosity; you are containing it.

Another effective exercise is the *narrative reset.* Instead of framing your investing system as something you "set and forget," reframe it as something you *commissioned.* Like an architect handing over a building to its occupants, your role is now that of overseer, not operator. You are not disengaged; you are post-engagement. This reframing preserves your sense of responsibility while releasing the compulsion to interfere. *Delegation is not abdication when the structure is sound.*

This mental reframing is especially vital in a world obsessed with novelty. Every day, a new headline, a new asset class, a new reason to panic or pivot. Trusting your system requires resisting the illusion of better. You must remember that every change, no matter how well-intentioned, reintroduces uncertainty. The moment you override your machine, you become the variable—and humans are notoriously poor variables. The more stable your system, the more your primary job becomes behavioural, not tactical.

To support this behavioural discipline, many investors find it useful to install a form of *accountability architecture.* This could be a financial advisor who aligns with your system-first philosophy, not one who markets frequent intervention. It could be a peer or partner who holds you to your own rules. Or it could be public commitment—declaring, in writing or to others, that you will not deviate from your plan except under specific, pre-defined conditions. This structure doesn't limit you. It protects you—from yourself.

Importantly, trust must also account for imperfection. No system is flawless. Mistakes will occur, allocations will drift, markets will do the unexpected. Trusting your machine doesn't mean believing it's perfect. It means believing it's *good enough to ignore until it actually needs attention.* This is a critical distinction. The lazy investor is not naive; they are appropriately calibrated. They trust their system not because it can't fail, but because they know it rarely needs fixing.

This mindset echoes broader philosophical traditions. Stoicism teaches that we should distinguish between what we control and what we don't—and act only on the former. Buddhism encourages non-attachment—not to give up caring, but to release the illusion that clinging brings control. In this light, trusting your financial system is not a technical act, but a psychological one. It is an expression of non-reactivity. A vote for stability over stimulation. A discipline that says, *the important work has been done, and the wisest move now is restraint.*

Yet even in this restraint, there is active vigilance. You must trust, but also verify—*on schedule, not on impulse.* That might mean an annual system audit: Are my auto-transfers running? Is my allocation still within tolerance bands? Have my goals or constraints changed? Once verified, you close the file. Trust is not passive acceptance. It is chosen consistency.

The payoff for this discipline is substantial. Not just in returns—though that often follows—but in mental clarity. When you trust your system, you reclaim bandwidth. You no longer carry the chronic cognitive load of daily decision-making. You exit the loop of reaction and enter the rhythm of process. You gain, as this chapter suggests, not just wealth but *emotional yield.* Time. Focus. Sleep. Confidence.

Trusting the machine you built is not the end of investing. It's the maturity of it. It marks the shift from building wealth to living in alignment with it. It's what allows your system to function like true capital—not just money, but a structure that does work *in your absence.* That is not disengagement. It is design. It is not reckless. It is refined. And it may be the most underappreciated financial skill of all.

Chapter 7
The Invisible Tax of Overinformation

At no point in history has the ordinary investor had such unfettered access to financial information—and yet, paradoxically, never more confusion. The modern landscape is saturated with numbers, forecasts, alerts, hot takes, and breaking news, all delivered with the urgency of a crisis. And yet, despite this apparent abundance, investors are not more successful. They are more reactive, more anxious, and often more misinformed. There is a subtle but profound distinction between being informed and being inundated—a line most only realise they have crossed when the cost becomes apparent.

This chapter confronts a counterintuitive truth that rarely surfaces in mainstream finance: more knowledge can make you worse at investing. Not because information is inherently harmful, but because much of what masquerades as insight is designed to capture attention, not enhance clarity. Investors today suffer less from scarcity than from overload. The hidden tax is cognitive, not monetary: each data point demands processing, interpretation, and mental filing. When your mental model is bloated with irrelevant or unstable inputs, decision-making slows, noise multiplies, and errors creep in.

Markets reward signal, not noise. Yet distinguishing between the two requires a discipline that is surprisingly rare: the ability to ignore. This goes against cultural programming. We are taught that awareness is power, that attention equals preparedness, that the "smart" investor is perpetually tuned in. In reality, the inverse is often true. The more data consumed, the more narratives to evaluate, the greater the risk of "narrative bias"—interpreting events through pre-existing mental scripts rather than objective reasoning. Illusions of understanding are far more dangerous than ignorance.

For the lazy investor, the remedy is selective ignorance—not apathy, but disciplined curation. It begins with recognising that most financial news is theatre, not journalism. Market tickers, daily forecasts, pundit debates: designed to keep eyes glued, not to improve returns. The attention economy has colonised finance, and urgency is its currency. In this context, silence is a rare and valuable asset.

This is not about hiding from reality. It is about learning to differentiate between information that truly affects long-term decisions—asset allocation, tax planning, life goals—and distractions that erode focus. The S&P 500's performance last Tuesday or a celebrity's tweet about crypto is not merely irrelevant; it is corrosive. The more one watches, the more compelled one feels to act. And action, without strategy, is almost invariably costly.

The myth of the "informed investor" deserves scrutiny. In theory, this figure consumes vast amounts of content, reacting nimbly to signals. In practice, they resemble a cat chasing a room full of laser pointers: distracted, reactive, endlessly chasing the next stimulus. Markets do not reward constant decoding; they reward temperament, horizon, and discipline.

The silence dividend—the cognitive and emotional gain from reducing informational noise—is among the most underappreciated sources of advantage. Silence creates space for long-term thinking, second-order reasoning, and dispassionate review. It allows investors to recalibrate, reaffirm fundamental truths, and focus on what truly drives compounding: low costs, diversified allocation, time in the market, and behavioural consistency. These truths are not glamorous, but they are effective. Clarity is found not in more news, but in less.

Practising information hygiene is not merely digital minimalism; it is a performance-enhancing choice. Boundaries are essential: disable real-time alerts, unsubscribe from clickbait, restrict market exposure to scheduled intervals. Cultivate internal signals as well: ask better questions, track metrics aligned with personal goals, and measure success by tranquillity rather than stimulation. By tuning out noise, investors tune in to their own reasoning.

This chapter presents frameworks for separating signal from junk. It critiques media structures that thrive on volatility and dependency, and offers alternatives to compulsive monitoring: rituals, heuristics, and simple system design. Strategic silence is not ignorance; it is liberation. The lazy investor benefits more from filtering noise than from anxious engagement.

Within that silence emerges intuition. External clutter diminishes; internal clarity expands. Patterns surface, priorities assert themselves, and time stretches. What seemed "essential" often turns out to have been habit, filling the space where calm could have prevailed.

The irony is stark: financial success is often framed as a function of brilliance—insight, timing, genius. In reality, it is more often a function of restraint. Not over-reacting. Not over-checking. Not over-consuming. Outperformance comes not from knowing more, but from interfering less. When you build a system you trust and shield it from noise, you create a sanctuary for capital—and for the mind.

This chapter is an invitation to reclaim that sanctuary. Not by retreating from knowledge, but by filtering it. Not by cultivating indifference, but by cultivating immunity to distraction. It is a manifesto for investors ready to trade the dopamine drip of headlines for the deep calm of perspective. Tuning out is not withdrawal—it is mastery.

Why You Don't Need to Know That

At any given moment, thousands of headlines are competing for the attention of investors. Breaking updates on central bank commentary, geopolitical tensions, quarterly earnings, analyst upgrades, commodity fluctuations, or the social media rants of celebrity financiers flood the screen in real time. Each one is framed as essential. Each one seems to carry the implicit message: *You need to know this, or else*. But here's the uncomfortable truth—*you probably don't*. Most of what parades as financial knowledge is, in effect, ambient noise: contextually hollow, tactically misleading, and strategically irrelevant.

The very design of financial media ensures this. Its business model is not built on your long-term returns—it is built on your attention. Platforms profit from engagement, not from accuracy or utility. This means the overwhelming majority of content is optimised for emotional arousal, not informational value. Fear and urgency are monetisable. Calm is not. As a result, the investor who passively consumes financial news without a filter is not becoming more informed—they are becoming *more anxious*, more fragmented, and more susceptible to impulsive decisions masked as rational responses.

To correct for this, we must begin with a foundational reframe: *the amount of financial information you consume is not correlated with your investing intelligence.* In fact, beyond a certain threshold, it is inversely correlated. Being selective—not omniscient—is the mark of the seasoned investor. The goal is not to know everything, but to know what *matters*, and to discard the rest without guilt or hesitation.

This requires a mental heuristic—an internal screening system that actively distinguishes signal from noise. A simple, yet powerful, starting point is this question: *Will this information change my long-term behaviour?* If the answer is no, it's noise. If knowing it won't materially alter your asset allocation, your saving habits, your investment horizon, or your risk tolerance, then it is decoration, not direction. It may be interesting. It may be clever. It may even be true. But it is not useful. *The lazy investor is not intellectually lazy—they are discerning. They protect their mental bandwidth with the same vigilance others apply to their capital.*

Take, for example, daily market movement reports. The Dow fell 200 points today. The S&P 500 closed higher. Oil surged on supply fears. These are classic noise items. They contain no durable signal about what to *do*—only shallow commentary on what *happened.* Even when explanations are offered, they are almost always post hoc narratives retrofitted to randomness. The market did X *because* Y. But correlation is not causation, and in finance, the map is rarely the territory.

Similarly, consider expert forecasts. Economists project interest rate cuts in Q3. Analysts predict a downturn in tech stocks. These sound authoritative, but their predictive accuracy is dismal. Study after study has shown that even top-tier forecasters underperform random chance when predicting short-term market movements. The illusion of foresight is an expensive one. Worse, these forecasts often lure investors into timing the market—a notoriously poor strategy for wealth accumulation. *The informed investor is often the most tempted to tinker. The lazy investor, meanwhile, wins by omission, not commission.*

The cognitive load of overconsumption also deserves attention. Every input you allow into your mind—every headline, tweet, chart, or podcast—must be processed, however briefly. This processing draws on limited mental resources. And while each item may seem harmless in isolation, collectively they dilute focus, clutter your decision-making process, and amplify the emotional volatility of investing. It's no coincidence that investors who check their portfolios daily report higher levels of stress and lower levels of confidence than those who check quarterly or annually. *What you consume controls how you feel, and how you feel shapes what you do.*

In practical terms, this calls for a disciplined information diet. Begin by narrowing your sources. Rely on a small number of high-signal, low-noise publications or analysts whose track records align with your long-term orientation. Avoid outlets that thrive on market panic, celebrity speculation, or incessant updates. Turn off alerts. Disable autoplay. Do not confuse activity with insight. Establish clear boundaries around your exposure to financial content, just as you would for refined sugar or alcohol. *You are not depriving yourself—you are detoxifying your decision-making environment.*

The heuristic can be extended further. Ask: *Is this information true, and is it timely? Is it consistent with the principles I've already decided on? Does it inform action, or simply provoke reaction?* Financial wisdom is rarely found in headlines. It is found in quiet conviction, built over time, rooted in tested frameworks and personal clarity. The investor who relies on external inputs for constant guidance is outsourcing their compass to the most volatile elements of the financial ecosystem.

It is important, however, not to swing to the opposite extreme. This is not an argument for wilful ignorance. It is an argument for *intentional discernment.* Some information *is* valuable—macroeconomic shifts that impact your long-term asset mix, policy changes with tax implications, or credible data that alters your understanding of a fundamental thesis. But these are infrequent and high-signal events, not daily occurrences. By resisting the pull of informational immediacy, you preserve your capacity to engage meaningfully when it matters.

The culture of overinformation also has subtle psychological effects. It creates a distorted sense of responsibility. Investors begin to feel that they *should* always be informed, always be acting, always be refining. This constant cognitive tension erodes one of the most essential ingredients for compounding: *patience.* If you are always reacting, you are rarely holding. And if you are rarely holding, your investments cannot grow. The paradox is that true informedness often looks like *inaction.* But in a culture addicted to drama, silence is misinterpreted as neglect. *The lazy investor sees silence for what it is: discipline made visible.*

To reinforce this mindset, it helps to adopt systems thinking. The aim is not to respond to each new data point, but to build an architecture that absorbs uncertainty over time. The less you have to *react* to external noise, the more your strategy can operate independently of it. Automation, predefined rebalancing schedules, and rules-based asset allocation all serve this goal. They allow you to interact with markets on your own terms, not on the media's.

Ultimately, financial knowledge is only as good as the behaviour it produces. Most investors don't fail because they lack facts—they fail because they can't maintain behavioural consistency under pressure.

Overinformation is a threat not because it misleads directly, but because it wears down resolve indirectly. It creates a background hum of anxiety that undermines rationality. *The mind cluttered by trivia is not available for wisdom.*

So, the next time a headline flashes across your screen—"Recession fears rise," "Tech stocks plunge," "Gold hits record high"—pause and ask: *Does this help me make a better decision today? Will this matter in five years? Will I even remember it in five weeks?* If the answer is no, close the tab. Return to your life. Let the noise pass. Your money doesn't need your attention nearly as much as you think. But your attention—scarce, powerful, finite—deserves better than financial theatre.

Because when you stop chasing noise disguised as knowledge, what you're really doing is protecting the most valuable investment tool you have: *your mind.*

The Myth of the Informed Investor

Few phrases are repeated with more reverence in financial culture than "Stay informed." It's delivered as self-evident advice, a near-sacred imperative in investor circles. Read the news. Watch the markets. Keep up with macro. Subscribe to this newsletter. Check that chart. In a world where volatility is constant and information is omnipresent, the idea that a successful investor must always be plugged in has become gospel. But peel back the sheen of conventional wisdom, and a more troubling dynamic emerges: *the more "informed" investors become, the more paralysed, reactive, and unsure of themselves they often are.* The cult of constant information does not create clarity—it creates confusion masquerading as diligence.

The myth of the informed investor rests on a seductive assumption: that access to more data equals better decisions. It flatters the ego and justifies the discomfort. The daily ritual of reading economic briefings or streaming financial panels feels productive. It scratches the itch of control. But underneath this veneer lies a toxic inversion—*information beyond a certain threshold stops being additive and starts becoming corrosive.* Not because it is false, but because it is fragmented, non-actionable, and disproportionately short-term. The investor consuming ten conflicting opinions in a day is not gaining insight—they are absorbing indecision.

What's more, most of what is categorised as "information" in the financial world is not built to educate. It is built to *stimulate.* Much like fast food is engineered to be addictive but not nourishing, most financial content is crafted to provoke without enlightening. It exploits the human tendency toward pattern recognition, fear of loss, and social comparison. This is not passive education—it is *performative anxiety.* Headlines scream, pundits debate, charts flash. And somewhere in the noise, the investor forgets what they came for in the first place: a clear, grounded, sustainable framework for building wealth.

Data supports this. Studies in behavioural finance repeatedly show that the investors who follow markets most closely often perform worse than those who check in occasionally. The DALBAR Quantitative Analysis of Investor Behavior, for example, has found year after year that the average investor underperforms the index—not because of bad luck or poor selection, but because of poor timing driven by emotional overreactions. And emotional overreactions are driven by overexposure to noise. *To be constantly informed is to be constantly tempted. And temptation, not ignorance, is the real risk.*

The modern investor is rarely making decisions from a clean slate. They are making them with a mental feed already saturated by tweets, interviews, opinion pieces, chart porn, and algorithmically curated alerts. Each one adds cognitive friction. Each one subtly shifts perception. Over time, this does not lead to better thinking—it leads to defensive thinking. The investor is no longer planning—they're reacting. And the result is a style of investing that feels exhausting: constant vigilance, high churn, low conviction. *The illusion of control becomes a substitute for actual control.*

To understand how this myth persists, one must look at its cultural roots. In most professional fields, information is indeed power. Doctors must stay current. Pilots must be alert. Engineers must monitor systems in real time. The presumption is that being "out of the loop" is dangerous. But investing is not like flying a plane or performing surgery. It is slow by nature. Its feedback loops are elongated. Success is not about real-time optimisation—it is about enduring with discipline. *In investing, the dangers are more often internal than external. The cockpit you must monitor is psychological, not informational.*

But this cognitive model is hard to internalise. The identity of "the informed investor" is socially rewarded. It signals sophistication. At parties, the investor who rattles off the latest from the Bank of England or quotes market cap ratios garners attention. The investor who shrugs and says, "I don't really follow the news, I just rebalance once a year," is met with scepticism, even ridicule. But the irony is sharp: *one is playing the game, the other is winning it.* True expertise in investing often looks boring. It is marked not by constant adaptation, but by intelligent constraint.

The solution is not ignorance. It is selectivity. The seasoned investor understands that knowing everything is impossible and unnecessary. Their goal is not to consume information reactively, but to design a system that filters proactively. What qualifies as useful information? It is timely, true, and tethered to a strategic decision already defined. If it doesn't meet that bar, it is passed over, no matter how urgent or viral it appears. *Discretion is not laziness—it is mastery.*

This insight has profound implications. It suggests that information hygiene—not just information access—is a core skill for the modern investor. Just as elite athletes monitor sleep, nutrition, and recovery, elite investors monitor the quality of their mental inputs. They do not let their portfolios—or their peace of mind—be dictated by headlines. They understand that tuning out is not withdrawal, but strategy. And they design rituals to protect that space: scheduled check-ins, automatic rebalancing, limited logins, or the delegation of monitoring to a trusted advisor. These behaviours are not signs of disinterest—they are signs of commitment to a long-term outcome.

Ironically, the cult of the informed investor thrives precisely because it feels so rational. Who wouldn't want to stay up to date? Who wouldn't want to anticipate market shifts? But this desire to anticipate often leads to anticipation *without preparation.* The investor is caught mid-stream—aware of every ripple, yet anchored to no shore. They see everything, but believe nothing long enough to act on it consistently. *Information is abundant. Wisdom is scarce.*

That scarcity is self-imposed. By chasing breadth over depth, recency over relevance, and novelty over principle, the investor becomes a prisoner of headlines. The deeper truth is that markets are complex, but investing can be simple. Simplicity, however, is not natural—it must be defended. And that defence begins by letting go of the myth that your value as an investor is proportional to the amount of content you consume.

So, the next time someone urges you to stay informed, pause and ask: *Informed about what?* Will this make me more consistent? Will it reinforce my strategy or derail it? Will it lead to better behaviour or just more thinking? If the answers don't justify the cost of attention, consider stepping away. Not forever. Just long enough to remind yourself that *the greatest edge in investing is not knowing more—it's needing to know less.*

Because once you understand that most of what passes for financial insight is merely financial theatre, the spell breaks. You see the myth for what it is: a distraction dressed as diligence. And in that space of silence, something powerful emerges—not paralysis, but perspective.

The Silence Dividend

If clarity is a competitive advantage in investing, then noise is its tax. Not a visible one, like fees or commissions, but a subtler, more corrosive kind—paid daily in distraction, stress, and misaligned decision-making. Modern investors are awash in financial content: live market feeds, investment podcasts, alerts from robo-advisors, YouTube analysis, Substack breakdowns, and newsletters penned by everyone from hedge fund managers to hobbyist speculators. There is no longer a scarcity of information—there is a scarcity of silence. And *in that scarcity lies the hidden cost.*

The premise that silence might generate returns is radical only because it counters a narrative deeply embedded in financial culture—that attention equals control, and that to be disengaged is to be irresponsible. Yet the opposite is often true. *Intentional information deprivation, done with structure and care, does not diminish intelligence—it sharpens it.* It allows signal to re-emerge from noise. It allows conviction to form independently of consensus. It frees up what is arguably the most undervalued input in decision-making: *emotional bandwidth.*

Silence is not about abstaining from knowledge. It is about reclaiming ownership over what inputs shape your internal state. In that sense, the real dividend of silence is not just better financial decisions—it is *psychological clarity*, the kind that lets an investor remain calm not because they know what's coming, but because they've built a system robust enough to not care. The paradox of modern investing is that most people are overloaded, yet underinformed. They scroll endlessly, yet understand little. They consume incessantly, yet hold no true conviction. *Silence breaks that cycle by replacing reflex with reflection.*

One of the most overlooked facts in behavioural finance is that the biggest mistakes often come not from ignorance, but from overstimulation. Investors act not because the facts demand it, but because the *buzz* demands it. Markets crash? Refresh the portfolio.

Fed announcement? Rebalance again. Bitcoin dips? Open the trading app. The average investor today behaves less like a long-term capital allocator and more like a dopamine-deprived screen user waiting for the next financial notification to justify an action. This isn't investing—it's *reactivity with a brokerage account.*

Intentional silence creates a wedge between the event and the reaction. It forces a pause—something algorithmic platforms actively work against. In a landscape where everything urges you to act quickly, silence is a rebellion. It's the investor saying, "Not everything deserves my attention, and not every movement deserves my participation." That distance—*that pause*—is not absence. It is a strategic form of presence.

This brings us to digital hygiene—not as a productivity hack, but as a foundational element of wealth behaviour. If one accepts that most market movements are noise in the short term and signal only in the long term, then the priority shifts from *monitoring change* to *enduring change.* And endurance is not just about portfolio allocation—it's about emotional architecture. A clear head is worth more than a clever thesis.

What does digital hygiene look like in practical terms? It's a shift from reactive consumption to ritualised, low-frequency engagement. For instance, replacing daily portfolio checks with a quarterly review. Or deleting market-tracking apps from your phone entirely. Or committing to consuming only one trusted investment commentary per week, not fifteen competing narratives per day. Or turning off financial push notifications altogether. These are not ascetic gestures—they are *design choices* to protect attention. They ensure that your inputs are coherent with your strategy.

The comparison with food is instructive. If you were serious about health, you wouldn't rely on whatever food landed on your desk at random intervals. You would curate your diet intentionally. Yet most investors do precisely the opposite with information—they consume whatever the algorithm serves next. *Unfiltered information is intellectual junk food: tasty, abundant, and often harmful in excess.*

Silence also creates space for intuition—not as mysticism, but as a refined pattern recognition that emerges only when the mind is not overrun with clutter. Every investor knows the feeling of reading an insightful essay or sitting with a strategy long enough for it to finally "click." That clarity doesn't arrive in the midst of information overload. It comes in stillness. Intuition, far from being the enemy of reason, is often its partner—*but only when given enough cognitive space to operate.*

And here lies one of the deeper arguments for the silence dividend: financial decisions are not just technical—they are identity-forming. They reflect your worldview, your relationship to risk, your tolerance for uncertainty, your capacity to wait. These are not values you discover through passive consumption. They are cultivated in quiet, when you are no longer reacting to someone else's opinion but interrogating your own.

There is a reason the most effective investment strategies are often the most boring. They are not designed to respond to daily events—they are designed to *ignore them.* Think of low-cost, globally diversified portfolios rebalanced annually. Or dollar-cost averaging across decades. Or value investing grounded in business fundamentals, not momentum narratives. These strategies work not because they are clever, but because they are *quiet.* They do not require constant reinterpretation. They require you to resist the temptation to tinker.

What most investors don't realise is that information itself has volatility. A new data point may shift sentiment wildly one day and reverse the next. Yet portfolios built to serve you in thirty years cannot be meaningfully re-evaluated every time a central banker speaks or an earnings report surprises. *The silence dividend is the return on emotional energy preserved, on decisions not made, and on mistakes not committed.* It is invisible—but no less real.

The risk, of course, is that silence will be confused with neglect. But these are not the same. Silence is not abandonment—it is boundaries. It is knowing when to engage, and when to step back. It is not detachment from responsibility, but detachment from noise. And when done well, silence increases—not decreases—your control over outcomes. Because it ensures that when you do act, you do so from *principle*, not panic.

In a world that trades in alerts and algorithms, cultivating silence is not easy. It will feel, at first, like ignorance. It may feel irresponsible. But that is only because we have been conditioned to equate vigilance with virtue. In truth, *discipline often looks like disinterest to the undisciplined.* Your silence is not evidence that you don't care. It is proof that you care enough to filter.

Investing, at its core, is a game of alignment. Between strategy and behaviour. Between goals and timeframes. Between what you say and what you do. Silence amplifies that alignment by reducing noise between signal and response. And in doing so, it unlocks not just financial resilience, but *emotional sovereignty*—a kind of inner calm that no headline can shake.

In the end, the silence dividend cannot be measured with a spreadsheet, but its effects are visible everywhere. In steadier hands. In longer time horizons. In less compulsive checking. In greater trust in systems you've built, rather than the stories you're told. It is not that the silent investor knows less—it is that they *need* to know less. And that, in a world overrun by noise, may be the highest yield of all.

Tuning Out to Tune In

The most overlooked source of intelligence in investing isn't hidden in analyst reports or embedded in predictive models. It lies within the investor—*not as a gut impulse, but as a cultivated, embodied awareness.* In a world saturated with opinions, data, and prediction models, what gets drowned out is the inner signal that says, "This makes sense for me." Tuning out, then, is not disengagement from responsibility—it is re-engagement with discernment.

Financial calm is not merely the absence of panic; it is the presence of internal coherence. That coherence cannot be bought, copied, or faked. It emerges when an investor builds enough stillness to feel the difference between fear-based decision-making and principle-based conviction. The ability to *hear yourself think*—a phrase once metaphorical—has become literal. And it's increasingly rare.

The modern investor is bombarded by external cues: flashing red tickers, macro commentary, Twitter threads dissecting every pivot, and headlines engineered to trigger urgency. Each input subtly suggests that you're missing out, falling behind, or about to make a mistake. This atmosphere trains the investor to outsource confidence—to treat information as a proxy for certainty. But *certainty that isn't your own is not security—it's dependency*. The habit of constantly checking markets, seeking confirmation from others, and benchmarking one's ideas against the consensus becomes a loop that starves the individual's own signal.

Learning to tune out is not a practice of avoidance; it is a form of self-trust under construction. It asks the investor to stop asking, "What's the market saying?" and start asking, "What do I know to be true based on my values, goals, and risk profile?" That shift is not easy. It runs counter to the cultural architecture of modern investing, where activity is rewarded and reflection is mistaken for complacency. But this recalibration is where meaningful strategy begins.

Consider the distinction between *knowing about the market* and *knowing yourself in the market*. The former is informational. The latter is foundational. Most people can recite the latest economic data. Fewer can describe how they react under stress, what financial freedom actually looks like for them, or what level of volatility is truly tolerable beyond the theoretical. Self-awareness is not a soft skill—it is the hard edge of durable strategy.

Embodiment is the bridge. While financial decisions are often treated as abstract mental calculations, they are experienced physically: the clenched jaw during a correction, the racing heart when an asset plunges, the tight chest at the thought of missing a bull run. These sensations are not irrelevant—they are *data.* To ignore them is to cut off half your intelligence. The most effective investors aren't those who eliminate emotion—they are those who *integrate emotion into their process with awareness and clarity.*

Tuning in means developing practices that anchor decisions in personal resonance rather than external consensus. That might involve journaling investment reflections weekly—not to predict markets, but to track patterns in your own thinking. It might include structured solitude, where each quarter you disconnect fully and ask not "How's my portfolio?" but "How aligned is my life with my financial design?" Or it could be as simple as tracking physiological responses when rebalancing portfolios—identifying whether fear or freedom is driving the choice.

Real-world examples illustrate this point sharply. Take the investor who religiously followed market trends but repeatedly bought high and sold low—not because they lacked information, but because they had no framework for *how* they made decisions. Contrast this with someone who checks markets quarterly, has a clear allocation strategy, and views money as a means of supporting a calm, focused life. The difference isn't education. It's orientation. One is tuned outward and reactive. The other is tuned inward and consistent.

There is a growing body of research around the neuroscience of intuition, suggesting that what we call "gut feeling" is not magical—it's the brain rapidly processing stored experiential patterns. Intuition, then, is not anti-rational—it is *subconsciously rational.* But it can only surface when the noise is low enough to hear it. Creating that space requires subtracting input, not adding more. It's less about being "informed" and more about being *available*—to your own internal models, developed through experience, failure, and self-reflection.

The value of internal signal becomes most obvious in market extremes. During bubbles, everyone sounds brilliant. During crashes, everyone sounds terrified. In both cases, external inputs become distorted. But the investor who has done the work of tuning in—the one who has interrogated their beliefs in calm periods, rehearsed their responses, clarified their endgame—is better positioned to act from principle rather than panic. This is not stoicism by force; it is equanimity by design.

This internal clarity also changes how an investor consumes information. It doesn't mean avoiding all external content. It means *being able to distinguish between signal and noise not in theory, but in practice.* The tuned-in investor reads an article and asks, "Is this relevant to my time horizon?" They hear a podcast and wonder, "Does this contradict or confirm what I already believe—and why?" The input doesn't hijack them; it informs selectively, filtered through an already coherent framework.

Tuning in also requires accepting discomfort. Silence is awkward before it becomes liberating. When you remove constant input, what surfaces first is usually anxiety, not insight. But this is part of the process. Stillness reveals the unprocessed noise we've been avoiding. Moving through that discomfort is how clarity gets earned—not as an intellectual abstraction, but as a felt experience.

It's worth noting that institutional investors often embrace this principle unconsciously. Endowments, sovereign wealth funds, and pension systems are often structurally designed to tune out—locked into long-term mandates, guided by policy statements, and shielded from short-term noise. Their success comes not from genius allocation, but from *infrastructure that protects them from reactivity*. Retail investors must build this infrastructure internally.

This tuning-in practice is also a powerful equaliser. You don't need insider access, complex spreadsheets, or predictive algorithms. You need the discipline to reduce input, the courage to sit with uncertainty, and the structure to revisit your thinking systematically. In that sense, *tuning in is not an edge—it is the ground on which every other edge rests.*

The invitation, then, is simple but radical: instead of looking outward for reassurance, look inward for resonance. Trade frequency for clarity. Swap headlines for personal heuristics. Replace urgency with patience. Let your financial life feel less like a reaction and more like a rhythm—one that beats in time with who you actually are, not who the market tells you to be.

To tune out is to trust that wisdom doesn't always speak loudly. To tune in is to listen anyway.

Chapter 8
Wealth Without Performance

For decades, the prevailing narrative in investing has centred on a single metric: outperformance. Whether measured against the market, a benchmark, or one's peers, the unspoken expectation is that a "smart" investor must always be ahead. Yet embedded within that assumption is a quiet but corrosive idea: if you are not outperforming, you are failing. This chapter challenges that notion—not by discouraging ambition, but by reframing the goal. What if wealth were less about returns and more about rhythm, resilience, and alignment with your life as it is actually lived?

To question performance is to provoke. It runs counter to financial orthodoxy, which has consecrated the chase for outperformance into a secular ritual. Financial media glorifies leaderboards; asset managers flaunt five-year alpha; retail investors compare returns online with the intensity of a global scoreboard. Beneath this hypercompetitive theatre lies a simpler truth: most people do not need to win—they need to stop playing someone else's game.

The statistical reality is unflattering. The vast majority of investors, professional and amateur alike, fail to consistently beat the market. Even those who outperform in one cycle often give back gains in the next. Chasing returns rarely works. The emotional reality is perhaps even more pressing: performance anxiety shortens horizons, fuels reactive behaviour, and erodes decision-making. It breeds stress and fragility, often manifesting as self-sabotage.

This chapter invites readers to step out of that mental race altogether. Not to settle, but to redefine. What does winning truly look like for you? Not in raw numbers, but in the degree to which your financial system supports the life you want to lead. This deceptively simple question becomes the axis around which the discussion turns.

Success, it argues, can and should be defined on personal terms: sustainability, psychological clarity, and alignment with values. For some, this may mean reaching a level of passive income sufficient to cover essential expenses. For others, it might mean the freedom to take sabbaticals, fund causes without external approval, or simply live without financial anxiety. Success is not what a chart declares—it is what your life feels like.

Reframing wealth in this way demands a new conception of "enough." Traditional financial advice—£1 million by 40, 25x annual expenses, 4% withdrawal—offers numerical targets, but often obscures subjectivity. One person's security is another's suffocation. Cultural norms, media portrayals, peer comparisons distort our sense of adequacy until we mistake more for meaningful. True wealth begins when the fear of scarcity yields to clarity about sufficiency—what is genuinely enough for you.

Psychology, particularly fear, shapes this concept as much as economics. Fear of missing out, fear of loss, fear of status decline—all magnified by an attention economy that monetises insecurity—can derail decision-making. The antidote is not mere discipline but introspection. Tools in this chapter help readers identify their own financial endpoint—not a figure to chase, but a condition to meet: one of calm, sufficiency, and coherence.

This is not a rejection of growth. Indeed, stepping away from performance obsession often produces better outcomes. Investors who cease trying to outperform can invest consistently, weather volatility with less stress, and avoid the behavioural pitfalls that erode returns. In doing so, they often end up wealthier—not only materially, but emotionally. Calm compounds too.

Illustrative examples abound: individuals achieving financial independence not through frantic trades or clever timing, but through structure, patience, and fidelity to personal goals. Their lives are quiet, systems-driven, and resilient. "Rich" is built not as spectacle, but as architecture. No drama. No fireworks. Just freedom.

The performance myth persists because it feeds a deeper misconception: that financial intelligence is about doing more, knowing more, optimising endlessly. Yet intelligence in this context is often stillness: recognising when to ignore, allowing compounding to work, having the courage to appear unimpressive in the short term in order to be unshakeable in the long. It is a message that sells poorly in headlines—but works.

Finally, wealth is perhaps best measured not by holdings but by feeling. Do you feel calm checking your accounts? Able to decline draining work? Present with those who matter, unburdened by performative ambition? These questions are central. Honest answers reshape the approach to money, revealing that the truest financial progress is quiet outwardly, yet powerful inwardly.

This chapter provides prompts to articulate values, define financial dignity, and resist the gravitational pull of more. It teaches how to construct systems that reward patience rather than performance. Wealth without performance is not retreat; it is purpose. It replaces external benchmarks with internal grounding, swaps status for sovereignty, and demonstrates that in a world obsessed with winning loudly, the greatest victory may be won quietly—on your own terms, for your own reasons, and measured by your own definition of success.

Redefining Success in Investing

For most investors, the starting line is already tilted against them—not by the markets, but by the metrics they've inherited. The narrative of modern investing has been hijacked by a single, unrelenting question: *Did you beat the market?* It's a question so pervasive that it distorts our understanding of what investing is for. Embedded within it is a presumption that outperformance is the highest expression of skill, and that any deviation from it signals mediocrity, if not failure. But this view, while popular, is intellectually shallow and emotionally corrosive. It turns investing from a personal system into a public competition. And more importantly, it misses the point.

To begin rethinking success in investing, one must first ask: *What are we optimising for?* Is it maximum return? Minimum regret? Lifestyle freedom? Intergenerational continuity? Emotional peace? These are not the same aims, and they cannot be served equally by a single definition of winning. The belief that one must always outperform assumes that financial success is a relative race. But in truth, the best investment plan is one that sustains itself over time, serves its owner's values, and grants more life—not more comparison.

Much of this thinking has been shaped by institutional investing culture. Portfolio managers are ranked quarterly. Mutual fund inflows are governed by recent performance. Hedge fund letters are written for applause. But for individuals—especially long-term, time-conscious investors—the stakes are different. Most are not looking to outperform in 12 months. They are looking to retire in 25 years. They want to buy time, not tension. For them, *sustainability beats sensationalism.* And yet, the culture of investing has been slow to accommodate this reality.

The misalignment starts with how we define risk. Traditional finance treats risk as volatility—as standard deviation from the mean. But for the real human investor, risk is not volatility. Risk is interruption. Risk is being forced to sell at the wrong time. Risk is losing the confidence to stay the course. A strategy that promises 2% more annual return but triples your chances of abandoning ship during a downturn is not superior—it is structurally unstable. *True risk is behavioural, not statistical.*

What then is a better definition of success? One answer lies in *coherence*—a state in which your investments align with your financial goals, your lifestyle constraints, your psychological profile, and your ethical convictions. An investment plan that does not demand constant tinkering, emotional exhaustion, or moral compromise is already outperforming—not in return, but in life utility. Coherence doesn't make headlines, but it makes freedom.

This broader understanding of success invites us to replace the language of winning with that of *fitting*. A good investment plan is not necessarily the one with the highest Sharpe ratio—it's the one you'll stick with through a bear market. It's the one that lets you sleep at night, ignore CNBC, and go for a walk instead of refreshing a watchlist. It's the one that funds your child's education without compromising your peace. Winning, under this lens, is not about more—it's about enough, consistently earned and quietly held.

Consider the financial lives of two hypothetical investors. Investor A obsessively chases alpha. She reads markets daily, toggles between ETFs, and holds a diversified portfolio of 50 positions. Some years, she outperforms the S&P 500. Other years, she misses. She spends significant time managing her portfolio, checking performance, and adjusting based on headlines. Investor B, meanwhile, holds a globally diversified index portfolio, rebalances once a year, and ignores news entirely. Over 20 years, Investor A might marginally outperform on paper. But Investor B outperforms in time, energy, and mental clarity. Which one really "won"?

To reorient success in this way is not a retreat into passivity. It is an assertion of agency. It is the refusal to be seduced by metrics that serve other people's incentives. It also invites a richer set of questions: *What does financial integrity look like for me? What is the minimum complexity required to meet my goals? What is the emotional cost of my investing strategy—and is it worth the supposed gains?* These are not soft questions. They are strategic ones.

There is also a deeper cultural dimension at play. We are conditioned—by media, schooling, and social comparison—to view financial accomplishment as a form of dominance. The best investors are the smartest ones. The smartest ones win. And those who don't win must be missing something. But this model is brittle. It frames investing as a zero-sum arena, where performance is a proxy for identity. The danger here is not just impracticality, but spiritual erosion. When your worth is tethered to returns, your peace is always negotiable.

A more robust model acknowledges that success is multidimensional. It includes time freedom, stress levels, ethical congruence, and legacy. And crucially, it recognises that *you don't need to win in markets if you win in your life.* This truth has been borne out in behavioural finance studies, which consistently show that the best long-term outcomes come not from perfect foresight, but from boring consistency. The humble 60/40 investor who contributes monthly and never flinches often outpaces the strategist who second-guesses the cycle.

This brings us to an important principle: *The best investment strategy is the one you can follow for the longest uninterrupted time.* Not the one with the flashiest promise. Not the one with the fanciest model. Just the one you can implement, stick with, and let compound. Because compounding is indifferent to your cleverness. It only rewards your consistency.

That's why this chapter argues for new definitions of winning. Winning as being able to go months without thinking about your portfolio. Winning as feeling calm during a market drop. Winning as setting your finances on autopilot while you attend to your health, relationships, and creativity. Winning as watching others panic while you do nothing. These are not minor achievements. They are signs of system design done right.

In practical terms, this redefinition requires tools and frameworks that serve the investor's life, not just their spreadsheet. Financial planning must expand to include qualitative indicators—sleep quality, partner alignment, career flexibility. Advisors and thought leaders must shift the conversation from beating benchmarks to building structures. And individual investors must learn to ignore applause and embrace adequacy.

The resistance to this redefinition often comes from a misunderstanding of ambition. The assumption is that stepping away from performance metrics signals complacency. But this is a false binary. It is entirely possible to be rigorous, intentional, and ambitious—while choosing metrics that serve inner stability over outer comparison. In fact, the most disciplined investors are often those who commit to simplicity with unflinching resolve.

Ultimately, this redefinition is not just a strategy—it's a stance. It is a stance that says: I will not let markets hijack my peace. I will not let relative performance define my path. I will not serve metrics that do not serve me. Instead, I will build a system that is coherent, sustainable, and rooted in values. And I will define success not by noise, but by nourishment.

By doing so, the investor steps into a new paradigm—one where the quiet accumulation of calm replaces the volatile pursuit of more. Where sustainability is not a limitation, but a superpower. And where self-worth is decoupled from screen performance and realigned with something far more enduring: the ability to live freely, wisely, and well.

Enough Is Not a Number

If you ask the average investor how much is enough, you're unlikely to receive a clear answer. You'll get a range, a guess, or a moving target. They may say, "A couple of million," or "Enough to retire early," or "More than I have now." But probe further and the logic crumbles. The idea of *enough*—something that ought to serve as a financial anchor—has been so thoroughly distorted by cultural cues, competitive signalling, and ambient fear that it no longer functions as a metric. It has become a mirage: ever-present, never grasped. And this confusion has a cost. Without a grounded sense of enough, wealth creation becomes unmoored from purpose. The finish line recedes, and with it, the possibility of rest.

The first issue is that most definitions of enough are externally inherited. They are not designed—they are absorbed. People look sideways to peers, influencers, colleagues, or social benchmarks and assume that adequacy is a function of where they sit in the hierarchy. If the neighbour buys a second property, maybe you're behind. If your friend retires at 52, maybe you've failed. But what is being measured in these comparisons is not sufficiency—it is status. And status, by its nature, is positional and insatiable. The more you chase it, the more it eludes you. *Comparison is a broken compass for defining enough.*

There is also a more subtle force at work: fear. In a world marked by uncertainty—economic, geopolitical, environmental—the impulse to keep accumulating is often rationalised as prudence. What if markets collapse? What if health expenses rise? What if I lose my job, or my partner gets ill, or inflation spikes for a decade? These are not irrational concerns. But when left unchecked, they mutate into hoarding behaviours dressed up as discipline. Investors convince themselves that more is always safer. But this safety is theoretical. It is the kind that never arrives, because it is tethered to future contingencies, not present realities.

We must be honest about how this fear-driven accumulation distorts our relationship with money. It invites overwork, chronic stress, financial anxiety, and often, fractured relationships. People miss birthdays, delay joy, and defer life experiences, all in the name of a number they haven't defined. Worse still, they believe that reaching that undefined number will suddenly confer peace. But *peace is a skill, not a milestone.* It is built through clarity, boundaries, and intentional design—not through endless accrual.

To reclaim the concept of enough, we must first reframe it not as a figure, but as a *function.* Enough is what allows you to live in alignment with your values, obligations, and aspirations—without dependency, distortion, or depletion. It is deeply personal. For one person, it might mean a small house, flexible work, and long afternoons. For another, it might mean financial support for ageing parents and robust philanthropic giving. But either way, it is shaped from within—not imposed from without. This is the work of financial individuation.

Practically, the process begins by defining what you *want your money to do for you.* Not abstractly, but concretely. Do you want it to buy freedom from a toxic job? To fund a sabbatical? To provide intergenerational stability? To reduce dependence on your children later in life? These questions force precision. They shift the lens from accumulation to utility. Once you are clear on the job you want your money to perform, the concept of enough becomes a matter of arithmetic—not aspiration.

The next step is to decouple the idea of sufficiency from the illusion of optimisation. Many investors assume that "enough" should reflect the *best possible version of their financial life*—the ideal home, the most secure legacy, the largest buffer. But optimisation is a mirage, especially when it's based on ever-shifting assumptions about return, inflation, and longevity. You don't need the optimal outcome. You need a *robust*, *sustainable*, and *non-fragile* one. The goal is not to outguess the future—it's to be able to withstand it.

There's a concept in systems thinking known as the "good enough threshold." It acknowledges that beyond a certain point, marginal gains are not worth the cost in complexity, fragility, or energy. This applies to money, too. Doubling your wealth might double your responsibility, your tax exposure, or your administrative burden. At some point, more capital doesn't improve your life—it complicates it. And yet, few investors examine the *diminishing returns of accumulation* with honesty. Why? Because they are rarely asked to.

To build an authentic financial endpoint, you must go beyond net worth and into narrative. What would it mean to stop accumulating? What behaviours would you need to unlearn? What identity would you need to release? Many investors have constructed their self worth around the activity of striving. Financial independence threatens this identity—not because it's harmful, but because it invites stillness. And stillness, for some, feels like vulnerability. That's why *knowing when to stop is one of the most underdeveloped financial skills in modern life.*

Consider a thought experiment: If all of your current financial goals were magically met today, would you feel relief—or panic? The answer reveals how much your financial activity is driven by purpose versus motion. For many, investing is less about the result and more about the routine. The act of checking, managing, and strategising provides a sense of control. But this control is illusory. Without clarity on what enough looks like, these behaviours become compulsions, not disciplines.

One of the most powerful exercises in this regard is a *lifestyle alignment audit*. Begin by asking: What are the non-negotiables in my desired life? Then ask: What would it actually cost to sustain these non-negotiables—without assumption, with real numbers? Map those costs to time, flexibility, geographic freedom, and emotional health. What emerges is a blueprint—not for optimal performance, but for meaningful sufficiency.

For example, a couple might realise they don't need a high-income city to feel fulfilled. They might prefer a quieter town, part-time work, and the ability to travel six weeks a year. Their number might be a third of what conventional retirement models suggest. Another individual may realise that their sense of security is more relational than financial—and that investing in family, health, or community brings higher returns than a 9% compound growth. These realisations are not reductions—they are refinements. *They bring money into orbit around life, not the other way around.*

There is also a moral dimension here worth considering. In a world of growing inequality, environmental instability, and social fragmentation, the endless pursuit of more can feel both tone-deaf and extractive. Choosing enough—consciously, not by default—can be a radical act. It asserts that wellbeing is not synonymous with accumulation. It creates space for generosity, time, and presence. And it models a different form of ambition—one rooted in sovereignty, not supremacy.

This does not mean abandoning growth. It means *redefining growth as a means, not an end.* When you anchor your financial strategy to a well-defined sense of enough, growth becomes directional, not addictive. You're no longer chasing abstraction—you're resourcing your vision. This shift alters every decision, from portfolio design to lifestyle pacing to philanthropic planning. It replaces scarcity with strategy.

Ultimately, to say "I have enough" is not a whisper of resignation—it is a declaration of wisdom. It signals that you have asked the hard questions, ignored the noisy ones, and designed a financial life that honours your values over your fears. It frees you from the tyranny of comparison and grants you the rarest asset in investing: *clarity*.

And perhaps most importantly, it restores a truth that modern finance has obscured: that money is not the goal. It is a tool. A quiet, powerful, and obedient servant—when you remember to tell it what, precisely, you need it to do.

Rich Without the Rush

The world doesn't lack examples of wealth. It lacks examples of wealth earned with grace. Turn on the financial media and you'll be inundated with stories of extraordinary outcomes—tech millionaires before 30, viral crypto gains, leveraged bets turned fortune. The narrative is addictive: fast money, high stakes, visible drama. It seduces us into believing that the only wealth worth aspiring to is the kind with fireworks and frenzy. But beneath that illusion lies a quieter truth—one rarely told, seldom celebrated, and far more relevant to real lives. *Financial freedom, in its most durable form, is almost always unglamorous, patient, and structurally sound.* The people who achieve it don't chase heat. They engineer calm.

Consider Linda, a mid-level software engineer in Manchester. For 18 years, she earned a good, but not extraordinary, salary. She maxed out her pension contributions, invested modestly in index funds, and bought a two-bedroom flat she could afford on one income. She never timed the market. She rarely checked it. She stayed the course, increased her contributions when she got promotions, and lived well below her means. At 47, she no longer needed to work—but she still does, on her own terms, because she likes building things. Ask her how she got "rich" and she'll shrug. "It was boring. But it worked." That's the point. *Boring, when sustained, is financial dynamite.*

Then there's Musa, a primary school teacher outside Birmingham. No side hustles. No inheritance. No financial windfalls. What Musa did have was an unusually methodical approach to budgeting, a refusal to inflate his lifestyle, and a deep aversion to debt. He read two books on investing in his twenties, opened a simple stocks and shares ISA, automated monthly contributions, and ignored the noise. By 55, he owned his home outright, supported two children through university, and held a portfolio large enough to generate a modest income stream. No one would mistake Musa for wealthy in the City. But he lives on his terms. He has time, dignity, and margin. *He is, by every meaningful definition, rich.*

What links people like Linda and Musa is not their income, asset class preference, or tax planning wizardry. It is their *structure.* Each of them built systems that removed the need for constant vigilance. They didn't seek alpha; they sought autonomy. And they achieved it through *repetition, not reinvention.* Their wealth did not arrive with a single decision, but with the compounding effect of small ones made consistently over time. And this is where the prevailing cultural narrative fails us: it assumes wealth is made by boldness. But more often, it is built by rhythm.

This is not to dismiss ambition or innovation. It is to *reframe excellence as consistency over velocity.* The mythology of rapid success distracts people from the very behaviours that produce lasting wealth. Most people do not lose because they lack intelligence. They lose because they lack patience. They spend years looking for a shortcut that would have been better spent *building the long route.* And by the time they circle back to fundamentals, they've lost valuable compounding time.

There's a quiet revolution happening among people who no longer want to chase the market. These are individuals who no longer measure success by outperformance or visible metrics. They've opted out of the rat race—not because they're lazy or cynical, but because they've discovered a deeper form of financial confidence: *the ability to stop striving*. These people may not dominate headlines, but their lives are often a case study in calm. They own their time, their choices, and their mental bandwidth.

One of the great advantages of this slow-build approach is its emotional sustainability. High-drama wealth creation often comes with high-drama maintenance. If your fortune is tied to a volatile asset, a speculative strategy, or a market-timing thesis, your attention is never free. You become a full-time monitor of your own financial narrative. Every piece of news becomes a threat or a thrill. This breeds financial fatigue. *When your wealth requires your constant presence, it owns you.* But when your wealth is built on automation, allocation, and alignment, it can support your life quietly, in the background, with minimal interference.

There's also a moral clarity that emerges from this approach. People who build wealth slowly are rarely extractive. They don't burn through teams, ecosystems, or ethics to get where they're going. Their wealth is often aligned with values—stability, integrity, simplicity. That's why many of them end up becoming accidental role models. Not because they tried to be, but because their example offers a counterpoint to the cultural noise. *They prove that you can be successful without being spectacular.*

This isn't to romanticise frugality or glorify austerity. It's to recognise that most people overestimate what they can achieve in a year and underestimate what they can achieve in ten. The goal is not to minimise ambition—it's to *right-size it to your actual life*. A person working a steady job, contributing to a diversified portfolio, living within their means, and avoiding lifestyle inflation can achieve extraordinary results over time—without the drama. But they must resist the urge to tinker, compare, or chase novelty. That requires emotional discipline, not just financial knowledge.

Importantly, there is no singular blueprint. What unites slow-build wealth creators is not identical strategy, but *a shared commitment to remove volatility from their own behaviour.* They know that their edge is not in predicting the market but in managing themselves. They install rules, routines, and rituals that keep them aligned. Whether it's a once-a-year financial review, a strict "no financial news" policy, or an automatic investment schedule—they create systems that are harder to break than to maintain. This is the architecture of resilience.

Even their goals tend to differ. While some aim for early retirement, others aim for professional independence. Some want geographic flexibility, others value caregiving freedom. But their systems are built around *personal definition*, not social comparison. That alone shifts their trajectory. When you're not measuring yourself against someone else's highlight reel, you get to move with confidence. And confidence, in investing, is more valuable than IQ.

The absence of rush is not apathy—it is restraint. To be rich without the rush is to have exited the scarcity script. You are no longer reacting to the headlines, chasing the market, or measuring your worth by acceleration. You're investing not just money, but your energy, in a way that produces *enduring calm.* In a culture addicted to urgency, that is a radical and powerful act.

And yet, perhaps the most striking aspect of these quiet wealth-builders is how unremarkable they often seem. They are not flashy. They rarely give financial advice. They aren't evangelists. But sit down with them, and a deeper intelligence emerges—not just about money, but about life. They speak in terms of trade-offs, not tactics. They think about time as a currency. They value margin more than leverage. They treat wealth as a means, not a marker. *They have built not just portfolios—but peace.*

This is not a story of deprivation. It is a story of design. To be rich without the rush is to have chosen your pace with care. To have engineered a system that holds—even when the market doesn't. To have realised that your most precious asset is not your capital, but your capacity to move through the world without frenzy.

And that, truly, is financial freedom.

Wealth as a Feeling, Not a Figure

What do you see when you close your eyes and try to imagine "wealth"? Is it a specific number in your bank account? A house on a quiet coast? A calendar with entire weeks unclaimed by meetings? Or is it something less tangible but more visceral—a steady nervous system, a morning without dread, a dinner that lingers because there's no reason to rush?

For too long, wealth has been narrowly defined as a fixed, external quantity—a numerical target, a net worth goal, an income bracket. The financial industry, much of mainstream media, and even self-help rhetoric have reinforced this abstraction: wealth as scoreboard. But beneath that surface lies an alternative view, one that reshapes our relationship with money and self. *Wealth, properly understood, is a felt experience before it is a financial fact. It is about resonance, not arithmetic.*

This is not to suggest that money doesn't matter. Of course it does. But our cultural default has been to collapse the idea of "well-being" entirely into the quantifiable: salary, investment returns, square footage, digits in a brokerage app. In doing so, we've ignored the harder, more meaningful question—how much is enough *for you*, and how will you know when you have it? We've inherited a vocabulary that's unequipped to articulate sufficiency in non-financial terms. So we obsess over accumulation, often without pausing to define its purpose.

To calibrate one's sense of wealth by feeling rather than figure is not a regression into sentimentality—it's a move toward clarity. A growing field of behavioural economics, positive psychology, and contemplative finance recognises that *subjective well-being is not perfectly correlated with objective income.* Studies consistently show that, after a certain point—roughly £60,000 to £80,000 in developed economies—additional income delivers diminishing returns on life satisfaction. But what continues to matter are autonomy, time affluence, relational quality, and personal alignment. These are the silent engines of real wealth—and they are largely untracked by traditional finance metrics.

Consider two investors. The first earns high six figures, has a broad portfolio, and tracks the market daily with a mixture of excitement and exhaustion. The second earns modestly, automates their investments, and takes long lunches with their children. Who is wealthier? Which one would trade places, and why? When wealth becomes synonymous with *how you feel in your life*, the hierarchy changes. The external trappings of wealth begin to look less definitive. The internal state—peace, clarity, spaciousness—takes precedence.

This reframe asks for a kind of self-honesty that most spreadsheets can't deliver. What are you optimising for? Are your financial behaviours aligned with the version of life you say you want, or with a model handed to you by algorithms, advertising, or inherited anxiety? Accumulation is not inherently bad. But accumulation without intention is just another form of clutter—material, psychological, or both.

A useful starting point is to replace the question "Am I rich yet?" with "Do I feel resourced?" *To feel resourced is to experience adequacy, capacity, and stability in the domains that matter to you—not just money, but also energy, time, creativity, attention.* It's an inner sense of sufficiency that doesn't demand constant proof. And crucially, it is renewable. You can return to it, revisit it, and rebuild it if lost. Net worth can fluctuate with markets. Internal worth, once cultivated, is more resilient.

For this kind of wealth, conventional financial planning is only part of the puzzle. What's equally required is a form of inner planning—a deliberate exploration of values, pace, relationships, and meaning.

If your financial strategy isn't grounded in personal clarity, it will default to cultural noise. This is why even high earners often report feeling insecure, behind, or overwhelmed. They're swimming in metrics but starving for meaning.

To move from abstract theory to lived practice, start with this prompt: *What would a wealthy day look like, without changing your income?* Describe it in sensory detail. What time do you wake up? Who are you with? What do you do first? Where do you put your attention? This isn't wishful thinking—it's design input. You're not fantasising; you're prototyping a life in alignment with your sense of sufficiency. From there, the question becomes: *What systems, decisions, or habits could make this feeling more common, more automatic, or more protected?*

This exercise alone can reveal how many financial goals are actually stand-ins for emotional states. Wanting "£1 million" may mask a desire for safety. Targeting "financial independence" might really mean: I want to stop working for someone I dislike. Behind the numeric ambition is often a value craving attention—freedom, creativity, contribution, rest. Once you surface the value, you can find more diverse, elegant, and efficient ways to honour it. Not everything needs to be bought or waited for.

Still, there's an emotional hurdle to this shift. Modern capitalism teaches that validation comes from external benchmarks. To anchor wealth in internal resonance risks feeling out of step, unserious, or naive. It takes courage to measure success by how regulated your nervous system feels or how aligned your spending is with your values—especially in a society that celebrates hustle, spectacle, and scale. But the psychological payoff is real: *less chronic striving, more present living.*

This isn't a rejection of ambition, but a recontextualisation. You can still grow your investments, optimise your cash flow, and expand your earning capacity. The difference is that those actions now serve a clearly defined *why*. And that "why" is not abstract. It is felt. It is alive. It becomes the intuitive compass for your financial life, pointing not just to accumulation but to coherence.

One of the most enduring myths in personal finance is that a number will one day deliver permanent peace. It rarely does. People hit their "number" and find the bar has moved. The market dips. A life event disrupts the plan. Or the emptiness they hoped money would fix is still there, only more obvious now that the distractions are gone. This is not a failure of money; it's a misunderstanding of what money can and cannot do. Money is a tool, not a substitute for inner architecture.

And so, the real work of this subchapter is not to help you "feel rich." It is to help you *define what richness means to you*, on your own terms, and build a life that reflects that definition with fidelity. Not performatively, but personally. Not for others, but for your own lived satisfaction.

To do this, consider conducting a quarterly "Wealth Alignment Audit"—a simple practice of asking:

– What have I spent money on in the last 90 days that felt deeply worth it?
– What expenses drained me, even if they looked good on paper?
– What am I craving that no amount of money has yet delivered?
– Where do I already feel abundance, and how can I amplify it?

These aren't budgeting questions. They are alignment questions. The kind that make your money life more emotionally intelligent, less reactive, and more designed.

Ultimately, wealth as a feeling is a commitment to sovereignty. It is about choosing not just what to accumulate, but *what to notice.* Not just what to earn, but *what to protect.* Not just what to build, but *what to feel while building.* This shift is quiet, powerful, and subversively freeing.

Because once wealth becomes a feeling—not a figure—you can finally stop chasing and start designing. And that changes everything.

Chapter 9
The Lazy Investor's Mindset Manual

Most people misunderstand what discipline really entails. They picture it as a rigid force—a constant state of tension maintained by sheer willpower. True investing discipline, particularly for the lazy investor, is far subtler. It resembles muscle memory more than mental strain. It is not an ever-vigilant inner drill sergeant barking through market swings. It is a posture of calm trust, forged not through hustle but through clarity. To invest effectively while doing less, one must first think differently—long before acting differently. And that begins with how you see yourself.

Identity precedes behaviour. It quietly shapes how we assess risk, react to news, and judge our own adequacy as investors. If you view investing as a battlefield, you fight. If it is a puzzle, you tinker. But if it is a system to be built and left alone, intervention becomes unnecessary. This chapter starts where most investment guides never venture: at the intersection of psychology, identity, and behavioural design. For the lazy investor, the hardest work is unlearning the notion that constant effort is required.

Our culture glorifies action. Buy the dip. Cut losses. Rotate sectors. Outsmart the next crash. This performance theatre is seductive—it gives the illusion of control. Yet history is unsparing. Research spanning decades shows that even highly educated, active retail investors consistently underperform passive peers. Not because of lack of intelligence, but because they overinvolve themselves. Motion was mistaken for mastery.

Inverting this narrative does not mean carelessness; it means conscious intent. The lazy investor is not inert—they are deliberate. They are not disengaged—they are disentangled. That distinction, though subtle, rewires the frame entirely. Stillness is precision, cultivated. But it cannot arise by accident; it must be rehearsed.

Mental rehearsal, a technique borrowed from elite athletes and performance psychology, becomes essential. The lazy investor must practise inaction. They must internalise the feeling of markets falling without the compulsion to intervene. They must familiarise themselves with the tension of deliberate restraint. When the real moment arrives—headlines screaming, peers panicking, prices spiralling—the nervous system must already know its response: nothing.

This chapter equips readers to approach such moments with intention. More profoundly, it reconfigures the premise: the investor's task is not to perform under pressure, but to construct a system where pressure is irrelevant. We explore how to transform reaction into ritual, define success through conviction rather than comparison, and anchor daily behaviours in a broader internal creed.

The Lazy Investor's Creed, introduced here, is not a list of tactics. It is a living philosophy. A distilled code reflecting the book's deepest assumptions: that doing less can outperform doing more; that simplicity, structure, and patience are underappreciated forms of genius; that the best investor is often the one most willing to leave the system alone. By providing a short, memorable set of principles, the philosophy becomes not just intellectually comprehensible, but neurologically accessible in moments of stress.

At the core is a challenging truth for high-achievers: you do not need to be smarter, faster, or more informed than others to succeed. You need only to stay the course while others falter. Most errors in finance arise not from ignorance, but from emotional mismanagement. The capacity to hold steady—not only through crashes, but amid frenzies, bull runs, and cyclical excitement—is arguably the highest form of investor maturity. It is not glamorous, but it is rare.

This strength is not innate; it can be cultivated. Through contrast exercises, pattern recognition, and exposure to counter-narratives, this chapter teaches readers to identify herd behaviour and detach from it. The goal is not contrarianism for its own sake, but internal sturdiness—to know when convictions rest on principle rather than fear. The lazy investor seeks not to outwit the crowd but to decouple entirely.

Stillness, when deliberately designed, becomes second nature. But design requires specificity. Vague advice—"stay calm" or "think long-term"—fails when panic strikes. This chapter delves into behavioural architecture, offering scripts, thought experiments, and rituals that buffer against instinctive reactions. Just as sound cybersecurity anticipates human error, a well-constructed investment routine anticipates emotional volatility and neutralises it in advance.

Perhaps the deepest shift is philosophical: seeing investing as stewardship rather than performance; honouring alignment instead of chasing alpha; managing self rather than outcomes. Markets are unknowable; values, habits, and heuristics are not. The lazy investor does not play someone else's game. They play their own, on their own terms, keeping score only by their own rules.

Practical tools follow for anchoring identity before tactic. How can behaviours align with values? How do you separate identity-driven decisions from reactive impulses? How do these identity statements embed so deeply that, even under stress, they activate automatically?

By chapter's end, readers will have more than a toolkit—they will possess a posture. A mode of being in relation to markets that does not demand vigilance, bravado, or anxiety. The Lazy Investor's Mindset Manual is not about apathy; it is about integrity—consistency between belief, design, and action, even when unobserved.

Mastery begins here—not with complexity, but with clarity. Not with tactics, but with temperament. If previous chapters built external architecture, this one builds internal governance. Until mindset aligns, every system remains vulnerable to sabotage—from your own hands.

The reader who completes this chapter will not merely understand what to do. They will know how to be: an investor who does not flinch, who does not chase, who trusts the system they have created. Such an investor avoids burnout, thrives in silence, scales by standing still—and wins not by outperforming the market, but by no longer needing to.

From Identity to Strategy

Every investment strategy, no matter how technical or evidence-based, is quietly governed by a deeper, often invisible layer: identity. It's not a concept many investors think to examine, but it may be the most determinative factor in how money is handled. Beneath every asset allocation is a worldview. Behind every financial habit lies a belief about control, discipline, success, or self-worth. And if those beliefs remain unexamined, the most rational plan will still be vulnerable to emotional sabotage. The Lazy Investor's path demands that we begin not with spreadsheets, but with the stories we tell ourselves.

Before you manage your capital, you must manage your character. That doesn't mean moralising your decisions—it means recognising that how you see yourself shapes what feels possible, reasonable, or risky. Someone who sees themselves as a lifelong "under-earner" or "bad with money" will unconsciously make choices that reinforce that script. They'll overconsume, under-save, or panic in downturns, not because of poor information but because their actions are trying to match a subconscious identity. In this way, financial strategy is not a starting point; it is a symptom.

This identity layer operates silently. Few people walk around articulating their investing philosophy aloud, but everyone is enacting one. Some view money as a battlefield, always under threat. Others see it as a symbol of competence, using every market dip or rise to validate their intellect. Still others—often the most sustainable investors—treat money as a flow to be structured and left alone. The crucial insight is this: *your beliefs about effort, control, and discipline will either support your system or sabotage it.*

Take effort. Western financial culture is deeply steeped in the Protestant work ethic, where more effort equals more virtue. This leads many investors to equate "trying harder" with better results. But markets don't reward hustle; they reward patience, process, and probability. The harder you try—checking charts, timing entries, reading every earnings call—the more likely you are to intervene unnecessarily. Lazy investing doesn't reject effort; it redefines it. *Effort, properly directed, happens in the design phase—not in the day-to-day.* You build a machine to think for you, not because you are lazy in the pejorative sense, but because you recognise your cognitive limits.

Similarly, beliefs about control warp strategy. Some investors operate under the illusion that with enough knowledge, they can control outcomes. This creates a gravitational pull toward prediction: forecasting GDP numbers, tracking geopolitical shifts, trying to front-run interest rate pivots. But control is a dangerous fiction in markets. The real power lies not in prediction but in preparation. Designing a strategy that survives surprise is more valuable than attempting to eliminate it. And preparation starts by loosening the identity-level grip on needing certainty.

Then there's discipline. It's widely admired, but often misunderstood. Many people view discipline as self-denial: the capacity to grit teeth and resist temptation. But in investing, true discipline is not about suppression; it's about substitution. *You replace high-friction willpower with low-friction defaults.* You automate contributions, preselect asset allocations, and structure rules that don't rely on moment-by-moment decisions. This approach is not only more effective—it is more sustainable. It respects the reality that discipline fades under pressure, distraction, or stress. Lazy investors don't try to be better people—they try to be *honest people* who build systems that don't rely on being better.

To shift from identity to strategy, the reader must first conduct a kind of inner audit. Not of numbers, but of narratives. Ask: what do I believe about money that isn't factually grounded, but emotionally inherited? Whose voice is present in my investing fears—parents, peers, media? What do I secretly think makes a "real investor"? Do I equate movement with progress? Do I believe that wealth must be hard-earned to be deserved?

These are not casual reflections. They are foundational diagnostics. Without surfacing these biases, one remains at risk of misaligning strategy with identity. And when the two are in conflict, identity always wins. If you build a strategy that assumes you'll act like a stoic when your deeper self panics like a gambler, your plan will not hold.

That's why the lazy investor's first job is not tactical but existential. To adopt a new financial identity—one rooted in patience, structure, and internal sovereignty. This doesn't require delusion or motivational affirmations. It requires a concrete re-narration of self. You are not someone who "tries to be better with money." You are someone who *designs around your wiring*. You are not chasing mastery—you are engineering margin.

Real-world investors who embody this shift look different than the archetypes glorified on financial television. They aren't the loudest voices in online forums or the ones touting double-digit quarterly gains. Often, they are quiet, structured, and disinterested in market gossip. They set up boring portfolios. They automate deposits. They check their accounts quarterly—or less. And they rarely change their plan because their identity isn't tethered to outperforming. It's tethered to alignment.

This chapter doesn't merely advocate behavioural awareness—it provides a practical scaffold for change. That means guiding the reader through the conversion of identity into systems. What does it mean to make decisions based on who you are rather than what others are doing? How can you anticipate your future emotional states and build buffers in advance? Which rituals reinforce identity-congruent investing, and which ones slowly erode it?

You will also encounter examples of misalignment: high-income professionals who never feel secure, DIY traders who obsessively rebalance, early retirees who can't stop tracking net worth despite claiming detachment. These are not failures of logic. They are identity traps. And escaping them requires more than new tools—it requires a new lens.

At the end of this subchapter, the lazy investor will understand that the slowest, most personal work—recalibrating identity—is also the most catalytic. Every spreadsheet, asset class, and rebalancing rule that follows will be sharper, stronger, and more serene because it rests on the solid ground of self-clarity.

Ultimately, strategy is just identity in motion. And when that identity is crafted consciously, your investing life becomes not only more effective—it becomes emotionally lighter. Because you are no longer performing. You are no longer hustling for reassurance. You are simply being consistent with who you have decided to be. That, in the final analysis, is the real edge: not knowledge, not timing, but *identity-informed alignment.* It is the rarest asset in all of personal finance—and the only one that cannot be copied.

The Lazy Investor's Creed

If your investing philosophy can't fit on the back of an index card, it's probably too fragile to survive contact with reality. Complexity may feel intelligent, but it rarely endures. Simplicity, on the other hand, is resilient precisely because it requires clarity. For the lazy investor, the goal is not to memorise strategies—it is to internalise principles. Principles that are portable, flexible, and potent enough to carry into any economic climate, across any life stage, through both calm and chaos. This is the purpose of a creed: to distil a worldview into something lived, not just understood.

The modern investor is surrounded by noise. Apps ping with market updates, podcasts dissect earnings calls in real-time, and newsletters flood inboxes with "urgent" takes. In this information-saturated environment, it's not knowledge but *anchor points* that prevent drift. A creed functions as a compass—not for where the market is going, but for where *you* are going, regardless of the market. It reminds you who you are and how you behave when your environment becomes emotionally distorted. *A creed is not a forecast; it's a behavioural firewall.*

A well-constructed creed also answers a deeper human need: the need for internal consistency. Without it, every new piece of data demands a new opinion, every headline a reassessment of strategy. You end up playing mental ping-pong, mistaking movement for diligence. But the lazy investor doesn't aspire to be reactive. The lazy investor aspires to be *principled*, not predictive. And principles allow you to be boringly consistent in the face of exciting uncertainty. That is the paradoxical power of this philosophy: the less you react, the more resilient your results.

Consider, then, what makes a strong creed. It must be short enough to memorise, but rich enough to endure stress. It must avoid jargon, not because simplicity is childish, but because it is adult. It must focus on what you *can control*—your contributions, your allocations, your emotional habits—not what you *wish* you could control, like inflation, interest rates, or geopolitical outcomes. It must emphasise long-term alignment over short-term applause. And it must speak to who you are becoming, not who the market thinks you should be.

Let's define the Lazy Investor's Creed in its core elements. These are not slogans. They are practices embedded in identity, compact enough to recall, strong enough to stabilise.

The Lazy Investor's Creed

I am not here to outperform—I am here to endure.
I do not chase trends—I build systems.
I do not watch the market—I watch my behaviour.
I do not trust my emotions—I trust my process.
I do not seek perfection—I seek sufficiency.
I do not time the market—I give it time.
I do not react to noise—I respond to signal.
I do not optimise endlessly—I automate intentionally.
I do not manage minute details—I manage core principles.
I do not need to win today—I need to stay in long enough to win inevitably.

Each line reflects a choice. Not a tactical one, but an existential one. A decision about how you wish to relate to your money, your mind, and your environment. This creed is not a commandment list. It's a mindset map. And it only works if it's lived—not quoted, not framed, not idolised, but *internalised and enacted.* That's why it must be repeated. Especially when you least feel like it.

When a friend is doubling their portfolio in crypto, and you're sitting in a global index fund at a -3% YTD return—repeat the creed. When a financial influencer posts a twenty-tweet thread on the "macro risks of dollar debasement," and you feel an itch to move to gold or real estate—repeat the creed. When the market drops 20% in a week and every fibre of your fear says sell—repeat the creed. *It's not there to make you feel better; it's there to make you act consistently.*

This kind of repetition isn't blind faith. It's what behavioural finance calls a "commitment device." You make a promise to your future self that you won't let short-term stimuli override long-term thinking. You give yourself structure, not as a prison, but as a scaffold. The creed becomes a psychological immune system: a small, spoken dose of rationality to fight off contagion from irrational times.

What's more, a creed creates continuity between moments of clarity and moments of confusion. The person who writes their investing philosophy in a state of calm is often not the same person who faces a bear market at 2am. You must assume this dissonance in advance. You must build a bridge between your highest financial wisdom and your lowest emotional states. That bridge is behavioural, and it starts with belief. A belief that your process is more trustworthy than your panic. That stillness is not passivity. That staying the course is not laziness—it is *elite-level restraint.*

And while the creed outlined above offers a structured template, its deepest value lies in prompting readers to *personalise it.* Ask: what do I want to be true of my financial self, not just when markets are rational, but when I am not? What are the tenets that I would proudly hand to my children or a younger version of myself? What statements remind me not just of what I believe, but *who I am* when I believe it?

Some readers may initially resist this exercise, dismissing it as soft or philosophical. But philosophy, when applied to action, is the ultimate edge. The creed is not decoration—it is armour. In a world where investing is increasingly gamified, dramatised, and politicised, having a durable philosophy is not optional. It is your moat.

As we proceed through this chapter, you will encounter tactical applications of the creed. You will see how it translates into design choices, default settings, and behavioural scripts. But none of those elements matter unless they are grounded in conviction. Not the loud conviction of arrogance, but the quiet conviction of alignment. That is what the creed delivers. It reminds you that wealth, when built wisely, is not a pursuit. It is a practice. And like any practice worth sustaining, it starts with a vow.

Rehearsing Stillness:

Under high-stress conditions, most people act. The Lazy Investor learns to *not* act. That isn't passivity—it's precision. In the domain of personal finance, the greatest risks are often not born from ignorance, but from overreaction. Panic sells low. FOMO buys high. The data is clear: market volatility rewards those who wait and punishes those who twitch. Yet in practice, doing nothing is surprisingly hard. Inaction feels irresponsible. It feels like cowardice. But stillness, when deliberate, is a deeply disciplined act. And like any discipline, it can be trained. This is where *mental rehearsal* enters the conversation—not as meditation, but as *preparation.* Because the moment of truth never arrives with a calendar invite.

To understand why stillness requires rehearsal, consider the way elite athletes train—not just physically, but neurologically. A gymnast doesn't visualise a perfect routine for fun; she does it because imagery practice activates the motor cortex in much the same way as the movement itself. Over time, the brain encodes calm under pressure as a *rehearsed reflex*. For investors, the parallel is obvious. Market crashes don't warn you in advance. They erupt. And unless you've practised standing still when every nerve screams for motion, you will act—and probably regret it. *Stillness isn't instinctive. It's strategic.*

The average investor, unlike the elite gymnast or concert pianist, tends to rely on raw willpower in high-stakes moments. But willpower is a notoriously unreliable asset. It depletes with fatigue, distraction, and even low blood sugar. The more sustainable approach is to embed stillness into identity and routine—*to become someone who does not flinch*. This requires rewiring not only behaviour, but belief. If you see financial calm as laziness, you'll break under pressure. If you redefine calm as courage, stillness becomes your edge.

One of the most effective rehearsal techniques is scenario visualisation. Instead of avoiding thoughts of a downturn, a disciplined investor imagines it in detail. You rehearse what you'll read in the headlines: "Worst day for stocks since 2008." You visualise the drop in your portfolio, the discomfort in your chest, the adrenaline spike. And then—*you rehearse doing nothing*. You script your reaction: no app checking, no trade execution, no phone calls to your advisor. You train the nervous system to recognise the stimulus and pair it with stillness. Over time, this builds an internal association: fear does not equal action.

Think of this as neural precommitment. When the crash comes, you won't rely on logic—you'll rely on practice. The same way a pilot trains in a flight simulator for engine failure, you're running drills for market panic. And just like a simulator, you must repeat it often enough to make it reflexive. Once a month. Every quarter. Before earnings season. Not to anticipate the next crash, but to *normalise calm under chaos*.

This practice is especially critical in a media-saturated environment. Markets today are inseparable from narrative. Financial journalism thrives on framing volatility as crisis. Social media multiplies the pressure with peer-driven panic. When a market dips 3% and your feed is ablaze with red graphs, it becomes harder to remember your plan. This is where mental rehearsal shines—not as an intellectual exercise, but as a muscle memory of *stillness under simulated fire.*

Of course, there are those who argue that doing nothing is irresponsible. That hands-off behaviour is naive, especially in the face of complex and rapidly changing markets. But this critique misses the point. Stillness is not ignorance; it is *pre-authorised wisdom.* It stems from having already made the most important decisions in advance: asset allocation, time horizon, risk tolerance, and rebalancing protocol. The heavy lifting has been done. What remains is the discipline to honour the machine you've built.

There's also a philosophical layer to consider. Many of us equate action with agency. If we're not actively adjusting, we feel like we're being swept along passively. But this, too, is a cognitive distortion. Just as a good chess player doesn't move every turn if the board doesn't demand it, a wise investor doesn't make changes just to feel involved. *Sometimes, non-intervention is the highest form of control.*

The psychological mechanics behind this discipline are worth examining. Human beings are wired to respond to uncertainty with movement. Fight-or-flight isn't just metaphor—it's evolutionary design. But financial markets aren't wild predators. They can't be punched or outrun. They require a *third evolutionary upgrade: pause.* Learning to be still in the face of financial stress is an act of self-authoring—a deliberate override of thousands of years of instinctual programming. And that level of override is not accomplished by theory. It is built through *ritualised rehearsal.*

One helpful tool here is what behavioural finance calls "implementation intention." This means planning *in advance* how you will behave in specific situations. For example: "If the market drops more than 5% in a day, I will not log into my portfolio until next Tuesday." The specificity matters. You're not just vowing to stay calm. You're giving yourself a protocol. And because it's pre-decided, you reduce the number of real-time emotional decisions. This is a cognitive lever for self-trust.

But it's not only about not acting—it's about *trusting that inaction is working.* That's a different muscle entirely. Especially in a culture that fetishises hustle and penalises passivity, choosing not to act can feel like sabotage. Rehearsing stillness must also include emotional validation. You have to train not just what to do (or not do), but how to *feel right about it.* This is the quiet foundation of longevity in investing: not just avoiding mistakes, but feeling inwardly aligned with that restraint.

Consider the example of a seasoned index investor during the COVID-19 crash of March 2020. Markets plummeted, news cycles screamed recession, and retail investors rushed to exit. But those who had rehearsed the drill—who had visualised the plunge, scripted their non-response, and committed to stillness—held their ground. Within weeks, markets began their recovery. But more importantly, those investors retained something far rarer: *confidence in their own emotional governance.* That is the real dividend of rehearsal—not just financial gain, but psychological sovereignty.

It's worth noting that this practice doesn't only apply to market crashes. It extends to euphoric bull runs, to IPO frenzies, to that friend who "doubled their money overnight." Stillness must be rehearsed in temptation as much as in terror. If you've only trained for fear but not for greed, your discipline is incomplete. Greed often wears a nicer suit, but it can be equally corrosive to long-term strategy.

Rehearsing stillness is not about numbing emotion. It is about feeling the full wave of stimulus—anxiety, excitement, FOMO—and deciding, through practiced reflex, not to convert those feelings into financial action. The feelings can be acknowledged, even respected. But they are not drivers. They are weather. And you are the ship's design, not the storm.

This is the subtle but profound shift that defines the Lazy Investor mindset: *Your edge is not in constant analysis. It's in calibrated inaction.* That edge is earned, not imagined. It is built not through more data, but through deeper discipline. And that discipline is forged not in the heat of the moment, but in the quiet repetition of rehearsal. You don't rise to the occasion. You fall back on your training. The Lazy Investor trains for silence.

And when the moment comes—and it always does—you will not be surprised. You will be still. Because you've been here before.

Holding the Line When Everyone Else Moves:

There is no more seductive force in investing than the crowd. The paradox is that we often overestimate our independence just as we are being swept along by consensus. Whether it's a speculative mania, a social media-fuelled hype cycle, or a panic-fuelled sell-off, the pressure to conform in financial behaviour is rarely overt—but almost always present. For the Lazy Investor, whose creed is built on consistency, patience, and low-intervention principles, this poses a subtle but profound threat: *how do you stay unmoved when everyone else is sprinting toward—or away from—the action?* Holding the line when everyone else moves is not just a test of discipline; it's a confrontation with human nature.

The first point to understand is that markets are not rational machines. They are emotional amplifiers. And most market participants—despite their credentials—are not immune to narrative contagion. When news cycles flash red, when talking heads predict doom or euphoria, or when your neighbour brags about doubling their net worth in six months, your gut doesn't respond with logic. It responds with adrenaline, uncertainty, and an almost imperceptible shift in identity: *Maybe I'm missing something.* That's the opening crack. From there, it becomes dangerously easy to override the quiet confidence of your system with the loud panic of the moment.

Much of this behavioural vulnerability can be traced to what psychologists call *social proof.* In ambiguous situations, we look to others for cues about what's appropriate. This is adaptive in many domains of life—but it's disastrous in investing. The stock market is not a fire drill. Seeing others run doesn't mean you should. In fact, crowd movement is often a lagging indicator. By the time panic is visible, the rational moment to act has already passed. If you are constantly reacting to collective emotion, you are participating in a momentum cycle with the least favourable timing: buying when others are greedy, and selling when others are scared. That is not strategy. That is surrender.

So how does one build conviction that resists this gravitational pull? The first tool is *contrast clarity*: you must know not only what you do, but *why you do not do what others do*. Lazy Investing is not an apathy-based model. It is engineered inactivity. That engineering begins with a core belief: *long-term outcomes are driven by systems, not spurts*. The average person you see chasing trends is operating on a short-term dopamine loop—trading not for wealth, but for stimulation, identity reinforcement, or social validation. Your contrast is not just tactical; it is philosophical. Where others seek excitement, you seek endurance. Where others optimise for novelty, you optimise for reliability.

Case in point: consider the 2021 meme stock frenzy. GameStop, AMC, and others exploded not because of fundamentals, but because of narrative virality. Traders convinced themselves they were participating in a democratic financial revolution. For some, it was fun. For others, it was financially ruinous. But the real lesson wasn't about stocks—it was about susceptibility. Many long-term investors found themselves inexplicably tempted. Not because they believed in the thesis, but because they didn't want to be left out of the *story*. This is the danger of momentum culture: it reframes caution as cowardice, and makes inaction feel like incompetence.

To counter this, the Lazy Investor must rehearse two things simultaneously: *emotional sovereignty* and *intellectual preparedness*. Emotional sovereignty is the capacity to experience FOMO, anxiety, or social pressure—and still honour your chosen system. Intellectual preparedness means proactively understanding the mechanics of bubbles, manias, and corrections—not to avoid them entirely, but to contextualise them correctly. When you know that markets have historically swung through irrational exuberance and brutal overcorrections, you stop treating every new swing as an anomaly that demands intervention.

Another key tool is the principle of *pre-committed thresholds*. You should have, in writing, the rules by which you allow yourself to act. These thresholds could include time-bound reviews (e.g. once per year), value-based rebalancing points (e.g. if my portfolio drifts 10% from allocation targets), or situational triggers (e.g. a major life change). Crucially, *social or market sentiment must never be a threshold*. You don't act because others are acting. You act because your pre-defined criteria are met. This is how you create insulation from noise. Not by resisting it emotionally, but by rendering it irrelevant procedurally.

But even with thresholds in place, there is still the mental burden of watching others "win" faster than you. Here, it's helpful to shift the metric of success from *rate of gain* to *likelihood of durability*. Most fast gains are unstable. They rely on timing, not structure. And most "winning" investors—especially in hype cycles—lack exit plans. They are rich on paper, but poor in process. Their net worth may spike, but their sleep quality often doesn't. The Lazy Investor's measure of wealth includes not just numbers, but *nervous system stability*. That contrast matters.

This brings us to the most subtle—but most powerful—conviction builder of all: *identity alignment*. When your investing model aligns with who you believe yourself to be, your resistance to external pressure strengthens exponentially. If you believe yourself to be a thoughtful, deliberate, principles-first investor, then responding to market noise with haste would feel like a betrayal of self—not just a tactical error. This form of resistance is not brittle; it is rooted. You are not simply holding a line. You are standing inside it.

Let's make this concrete. Imagine a market drop of 12% over five days. Headlines scream "historic collapse." Your peer group is selling or rebalancing or tweeting frantically. You feel the anxiety rise. But because you have trained mentally for this, you do three things automatically. First, you consult your investing playbook—your allocation is still in bounds. Second, you remind yourself of your purpose: your financial system is not built for quarterly returns but for multi-decade utility. Third, you note the emotional cues and consciously do *nothing*. Not because you don't care. But because you *care in the right direction*—about alignment, not appearance.

There's a broader lesson here, too. Markets, like crowds, are built on short feedback loops. Prices move quickly. Narratives shift hourly. But wisdom has longer loops. The Lazy Investor is not trying to *win the moment*. She is trying to *remain coherent over time*. That is an entirely different objective. And it is rarely rewarded with public praise. In fact, you must be prepared to appear slow, outdated, or even foolish for long periods. That is the cost of conviction. But it is also the price of independence.

To support this conviction practically, it's worth periodically engaging in *retrospective simulation*. Go back to moments when the crowd panicked—COVID-19 crash, 2008, the dot-com bust—and walk yourself through what a Lazy Investor would have done. Compare that to what most people did. Observe the gap in results. Not just financial outcomes, but stress outcomes. This retrospective reinforcement makes it easier to trust your strategy when the next panic arrives.

Ultimately, holding the line is not a single heroic act. It is a repeated act of non-heroism. It is mundane. It is unsexy. It often feels like ignoring a party everyone else is attending. But you are not investing for applause. You are investing for sovereignty. And sovereignty, in a world of market mimicry, is its own form of wealth.

What we are talking about is not merely behavioural finance. It is *behavioural authorship*. You are choosing to write your own script, instead of reading from the market's teleprompter. That's not laziness. That's design. The Lazy Investor does not move with the crowd because their wealth does not require spectacle. It requires silence, patience, and the quiet confidence to keep walking a straight line while the world zigzags around you.

Hold the line. Not because it's dramatic. But because *it's enough.*

Conclusion
The Beautiful Boredom of Wealth

There is a peculiar irony embedded in the way modern culture portrays wealth: the more we consume financial content, the more we conflate money with drama. Markets are presented like sporting events, investing is marketed as adventure, and traders are cast as protagonists navigating a saga of timing, hustle, and strategic brilliance. This language—always urgent, often romantic—turns wealth-building into spectacle. Yet genuine wealth has little to do with spectacle. Its truest form emerges not in adrenaline, volatility, or the thrill of gains, but in their absence. It resides in stillness, in quiet, in patience. The lesson rarely taught—because it does not sell headlines, courses, or products—is that the pinnacle of financial maturity is boredom.

The profound boredom of wealth is not a flaw to be fixed. It is a signal that your money is working quietly, persistently, and without your constant interference. It marks a victory over the ego's urge to optimise, outperform, or prove itself. The system you have constructed becomes robust, aligned with your values, and independent of daily emotion, thriving without your constant attention. Paradoxically, what outsiders might mistake for stagnation is, in fact, the summit.

Reaching this stage requires a subtle psychological shift. One must stop being entertained by finances. This is deceptively difficult. Much of modern investing is tied to identity performance. We want our portfolios to reflect cleverness, decisiveness, and control. Boredom challenges this self-image. It feels like surrender. It feels—at least to the untrained ego—like laziness.

Yet those who are truly wealthy in both capital and calm are often those who intervene least. They do not check markets daily, pore over earnings reports, track central bank commentary, or scrutinise analyst forecasts. They do not rebalance impulsively or benchmark obsessively against peers. Their wealth has become infrastructural—more plumbing than performance. It supports their lives rather than directing them.

This is not complacency. It is clarity. These investors are not disengaged—they are strategically disengaged from noise. They have built a system capable of sustaining their intent without constant micro-adjustment. That is what renders their wealth boring—and what makes that boredom beautiful. It is not a lack of ambition, but the arrival of enough.

In this final chapter, we treat boredom not as a lull, but as a feature of financial design. It is a compass, signalling equilibrium in decisions, structures, and attitudes. We explore why most investors resist boredom, often unconsciously, and how that resistance undermines long-term results. We confront a question that underlies countless mistakes: why feel compelled to act, when inaction often serves better?

Boredom, when misinterpreted, drives unnecessary complexity. Investors layer strategies not because the system demands it, but because identity craves engagement. They optimise not because the outcome requires it, but because stillness feels intolerable. This creates a feedback loop: complexity breeds confusion, confusion breeds doubt, doubt spurs action that feels productive but erodes efficiency. The remedy is a countercultural embrace of what appears as disengagement—but is actually disciplined restraint.

There is a philosophical dimension as well. Our culture worships stimulation, rendering boredom taboo. We equate it with wasted potential. Yet boredom, properly understood, often signals internal calm and external sufficiency. In a world where constant striving masquerades as self-worth, the ability to live without urgent goals—to wake without financial anxiety or portfolio drama—is a profound form of wealth. Not wealth as accumulation, but as stability. Wealth as quiet freedom.

This chapter guides readers to recognise when they have arrived at this state and what to do upon arrival. Prompts encourage reflection: how much of your financial behaviour stems from fear or identity maintenance? Are you investing out of necessity, or from uncertainty about who you are without it? Can you distinguish genuine improvement from restless tinkering? We explore ritual, mindfulness, and philosophical clarity as anchors through quiet seasons.

Importantly, this is not a call to shirk responsibility. The lazy investor does not ignore money; they engineer it to require less attention. This chapter redefines the finish line, suggesting that the ultimate goal of investing is not dominance, performance, or optimisation—but peace. Peace, paradoxically, is often experienced as boredom.

So, if you find yourself checking your portfolio less, reacting to market news less, thinking about money less—good. If your wealth is rarely discussed, not from secrecy but because it is settled—better. If your financial life feels calm to the point of dullness, you are not off course. You are walking a narrow path few notice, but many secretly desire: a life where money no longer demands attention because it already mirrors your values.

This is what it means to be rich without busyness. Wealth without performance. Success without spectacle. The beautiful boredom of wealth. Perhaps the most radical idea in finance of all.

The Beautiful Boredom of Wealth:

The most subversive truth in modern finance is this: real wealth is boring. Not temporarily, not in contrast to something more exciting, but as a persistent, structural feature of its maturity. The excitement we so often associate with investing—the thrill of watching markets move, the rush of tactical plays, the dopamine of beating benchmarks—is not a feature of wealth. It's a residue of insecurity, performance anxiety, and unresolved ego. The more evolved your relationship with money becomes, the less you need it to stimulate you. The more powerful wealth grows, the quieter it tends to be.

That quiet, though often misread, is not a lull. It is a signal. It tells you that the structure you've built—through patience, discipline, and unsexy consistency—has begun to operate without your emotional sponsorship. The engine no longer requires you to push. It hums. What the novice investor mistakes as disengagement is, in fact, mastery. The absence of action is not laziness; it's control. And the absence of spectacle is not stagnation; it's peace.

This runs counter to the dominant mythos of modern wealth. We are surrounded by narratives of financial heroism: bold bets, contrarian timing, viral charts, charismatic gurus proclaiming the next big opportunity. Wealth is dramatised, aestheticised, and constantly *externalised.* It's no wonder then that so many investors grow addicted not to money, but to the *performance* of investing. They need to feel clever. Active. Superior. The market becomes a stage upon which they assert identity. But wealth built on this foundation is fragile. It may grow numerically, but it is structurally dependent on the investor's ongoing emotional engagement. Which is precisely what good investing seeks to eliminate.

The hallmark of true wealth is not how hard you work for it. It's how little it requires from you. The beauty of boredom lies in its resistance to performance. It offers nothing to flaunt, nothing to optimise, and nothing to explain. It is self-contained. This creates a conceptual tension: how do you calibrate your internal compass to value what feels, at first, like absence? How do you learn to respect *stillness* as a result rather than a void?

This reframing begins with the ego. Ego is not arrogance; it is the internal narrator that always seeks relevance. Ego does not tolerate silence because silence has no mirrors. Boredom, from the ego's perspective, is unbearable because it signals a loss of perceived control or validation. This is why so many investors, having achieved sufficiency, continue to tweak, trade, or tinker—not to improve outcomes, but to reaffirm identity. They say they are refining strategy, but what they're really doing is avoiding stillness.

The antidote is not asceticism or detachment. It is recognition. You must learn to *interpret* boredom differently. What feels like stagnation is often your system functioning as designed. What feels like disconnection is really freedom. The very lack of stimulation is a by-product of security. This is a feature of mature systems everywhere: a well-built dam does not leak. A reliable furnace does not flicker. A sound financial structure does not surprise you. If your portfolio is calm to the point of dullness, you are probably doing something right.

This insight becomes even more important in a culture saturated by novelty. The financial media economy is built to agitate—through predictions, narratives, and visualised volatility. Boredom doesn't sell. So silence is constantly interrupted by manufactured urgency. You are told that sitting still is naive, that disengagement is irresponsible, and that if you're not adapting daily, you're falling behind. But wealth does not move at the speed of headlines. It compounds at the speed of trust and time. A good investor must be *bored enough* to let compounding do its work.

Consider the psychological demands of this posture. To do nothing—when the crowd is moving, when headlines scream, when your peers are shifting—is not passive. It is an act of disciplined refusal. It requires a mindset trained not just to resist noise, but to be at peace with its own stillness. You must cultivate mental stillness not as an occasional tactic but as a way of relating to your money. This is a practice. Like meditation, it involves recognising the impulse to act and choosing to observe it without indulging it. Over time, this becomes not only easier but pleasurable. Stillness becomes a home state.

The deeper reward is that your financial life no longer demands constant attention. You free up cognitive real estate. You liberate emotional bandwidth. You become available to other things—relationships, ideas, creativity, presence. Money becomes the *least* interesting thing about your day. And this, ironically, is when wealth begins to serve its highest purpose—not as a source of excitement, but as a platform for *being*.

The economic philosopher John Maynard Keynes once wrote about the "euthanasia of the rentier"—a prediction that those who live off capital would eventually disappear as their role became functionally obsolete. But he may have misread the psychological adaptation. The modern "rentier" doesn't vanish—they transform. They don't disappear, they *disengage*. The most successful long-term investors are those who have made peace with boredom. They have stopped narrating their portfolios. They have stopped interpreting each movement as meaningful. They have stopped expecting their investments to do anything other than *compound quietly*.

This is a hard-won mindset. It requires you to override not just culture, but biology. Humans evolved to act under threat. Financial stillness can feel like vulnerability. But once internalised, the Lazy Investor's ethos becomes more than just a strategy. It becomes a worldview. One where excitement is not a signal of opportunity but a red flag. One where the absence of novelty is evidence of resilience. One where peace, not performance, is the ultimate benchmark.

Let us not mistake this as complacency. Boredom is not the *end* of financial mastery. It is its *climax*. It is the point at which your system has been so well designed, and your self-worth so thoroughly decoupled from noise, that you no longer need the market to entertain you. You no longer need money to narrate your identity. You no longer need external movement to feel internal security. You've reached a place where financial life is no longer a performance but a platform—stable, sufficient, and sustainable.

The final victory in investing is not winning more. It is needing less. Not because you have settled, but because you have refined. What's left is not emptiness. It's space. Space to live, to think, to choose deliberately. The boredom of wealth is not hollow. It is *full of margin*. Margin for missteps. Margin for health. Margin for slowness. This kind of wealth does not announce itself. It does not shimmer. But it lasts.

And in that silence—steady, uneventful, peaceful—you finally find what so many seek in the noise: freedom.

About the Author

Elliot Wren writes at the intersection of money, meaning, and mental clarity. With a lifelong curiosity about why we chase what we chase—and what we might gain by stopping—Elliot explores how simplicity can outperform struggle, especially in a world obsessed with more. A quiet advocate of doing less, he's spent years studying behavioral finance, minimalist living, and the emotional roots of money decisions. His work invites readers to step off the treadmill of financial anxiety and into a philosophy of deliberate calm. When he's not writing, Elliot lives slowly, reads widely, and checks his portfolio rarely.

www.ingramcontent.com/pod-product-compliance
Lightning Source LLC
Chambersburg PA
CBHW031349230926
51848CB00002B/445